THE LAST MAN — Unmanned

Brian K. Vaughan
Writer

Pia Guerra
Penciller

José Marzán, Jr.
Inker

Pamela Rambo
Colorist

Clem Robins
Letterer

J.G. Jones
Original series covers

Y: THE LAST MAN created by Brian K. Vaughan and Pia Guerra

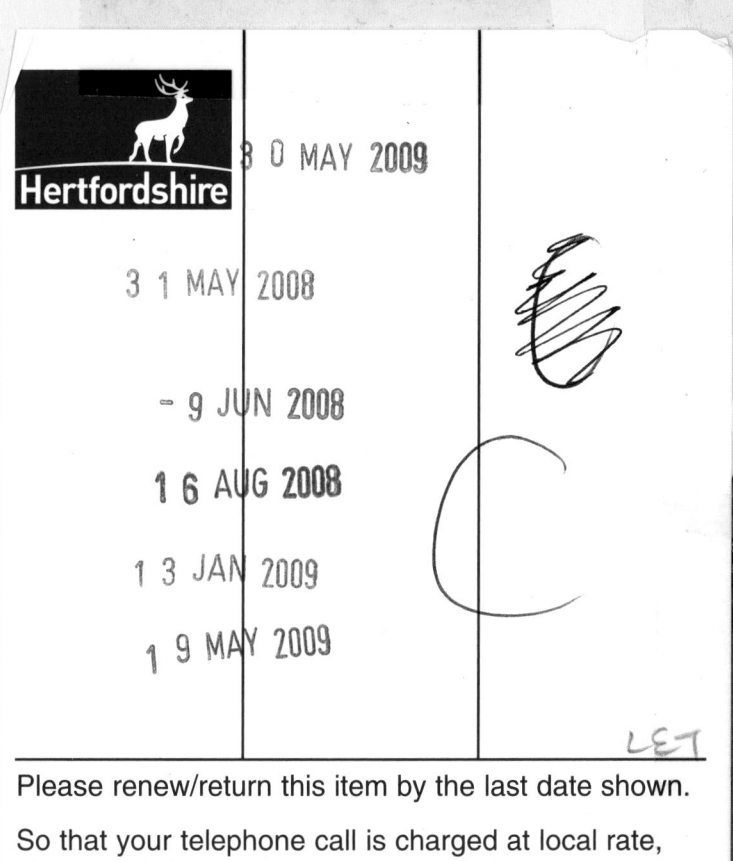
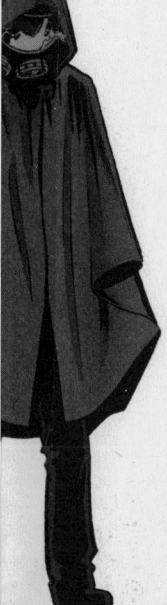

Karen Berger
VP-Executive Editor

Heidi MacDonald
Steve Bunche
Editors-original series

Zachary Rau
Assistant Editor-original series

Scott Nybakken
Editor-collected edition

Robbin Brosterman
Senior Art Director

Paul Levitz
President & Publisher

Georg Brewer
VP-Design & DC Direct Creative

Richard Bruning
Senior VP-Creative Director

Patrick Caldon
Senior VP-Finance & Operations

Chris Caramalis
VP-Finance

Terri Cunningham
VP-Managing Editor

Stephanie Fierman
Senior VP-Sales & Marketing

Alison Gill
VP-Manufacturing

Rich Johnson
VP-Book Trade Sales

Hank Kanalz
VP-General Manager, WildStorm

Lillian Laserson
Senior VP & General Counsel

Jim Lee
Editorial Director-WildStorm

Paula Lowitt
Senior VP-Business & Legal Affairs

David McKillips
VP-Advertising & Custom Publishing

John Nee
VP-Business Development

Gregory Noveck
Senior VP-Creative Affairs

Cheryl Rubin
Senior VP-Brand Management

Jeff Trojan
VP-Business Development, DC Direct

Bob Wayne
VP-Sales

Y: THE LAST MAN — UNMANNED

DC Comics, 1700 Broadway, New York, NY 10019
A Warner Bros. Entertainment Company
Printed in Canada. Fifth Printing.
ISBN: 1-56389-980-9
Cover illustration by J.G. Jones.
Publication design by Louis Prandi.
Logo design by Terry Marks.

Brooklyn, New York
Now

Brooklyn, New York
Twenty-Nine Minutes Ago

YORICK, IT COSTS SEVENTY-FIVE CENTS A MINUTE TO CALL THE OUTBACK.

DO YOU REALLY WANNA CHAT ABOUT *ELVIS*?

MONEY IS *NOT A CONCERN*, BETH. AFTER ALL, I'M TALKING TO MY BELOVED SNUGGLE PANTS, NOT SOME PHONE SEX WHORE.

BESIDES, MY SISTER GAVE ME A PHONE CARD FOR CHRISTMAS...

ANYWAY, DID YOU KNOW...

...THAT ELVIS HAD A TWIN BROTHER? NO. WHERE DID YOU READ THIS, THE *ENQUIRER*?

IT'S TRUE! AN *IDENTICAL* TWIN BROTHER!

HIS NAME WAS JESSE GARON PRESLEY, STILLBORN A FEW MINUTES BEFORE GLADYS GAVE BIRTH TO THE KING. THEY BURIED HIM IN A *SHOE-BOX*.

HOW *INSANE* IS THAT? I MEAN. WHAT IF JESSE HAD LIVED AND *ELVIS* HAD DIED? OR... OR WHAT IF THEY HAD *BOTH* LIVED?

YORICK, YOU DON'T EVEN LIKE ELVIS. WHERE THE HELL IS THIS COMING FROM?

I DON'T KNOW. DO YOU EVER THINK ABOUT *DESTINY*?

WHY DOES FATE CHOOSE ONE MAN OVER ANOTHER, THAT SORTA THING...?

YOU DIDN'T GET THE JOB, DID YOU?

uh, NO.

NO, I DIDN'T.

I'M SORRY, BABY.

BUT YOU'LL FIND SOMETHING ELSE! YOU'VE JUST GOT TO GIVE IT A LITTLE TIME.

MAYBE... BUT I GRADUATED MORE THAN A *YEAR* AGO, BETH, AND THE JOB MARKET ISN'T EXACTLY *BOOMING* FOR ENGLISH MAJORS WITH MODERATE-TO-POOR COMPUTER SKILLS.

ARE YOU OKAY FOR CASH, AT LEAST?

YEAH, I'LL BE KICKIN' IT RAMEN-NOODLE STYLE FOR A MONTH, BUT I SHOULD BE ABLE TO MAKE RENT.

I SCORED A COUPLE HUNDRED BUCKS DOING LAME-ASS CARD TRICKS IN WASHINGTON SQUARE YESTERDAY, BUT A COP MADE ME GIVE HIM *HALF* 'CAUSE I BORROWED HIS HANDCUFFS FOR AN ESCAPE.

A COP! I SWEAR, IT WAS LIKE *BAD LIEUTENANT* OR SOMETHING. I'M THINKING ABOUT REPORTING HIM TO THE ≿KLICK≾ FOR SHAKING DOWN ≿KLICK≾

CRAP, I'VE GOT CALL WAITING. CAN YOU HOLD ON A SECOND?

IT'S YOUR PHONE CARD, SERPICO.

THANKS, DON'T GO AWAY...

HELLO?

DID YOU GET THE JOB, SWEETIE?

HEY, MOM.

Washington, D.C.
Twenty-Four Minutes Ago

Um, I'VE ACTUALLY GOT BETH ON THE OTHER LINE. CAN WE TALK ABOUT THIS LATER?

OF COURSE, YORICK. PLEASE SEND BETHIE MY LOVE.

AND DON'T FORGET TO CALL YOUR FATHER FOR HIS BIRTHDAY. HE HAS THAT MARLOWE CLASS TONIGHT, BUT HE'LL BE HOME FOR HIS PARTY AT EIGHT. BYE, NOW!

DID HE GET THE JOB, MA'AM?

DIDN'T SOUND LIKE IT, NO.

CONGRESS-WOMAN BROWN!

SENATOR, WHAT A TREAT.

AND IF YOU DON'T MIND, I PREFER *REPRESENTATIVE* BROWN. TWENTY-FIRST CENTURY AND ALL THAT.

MY APOLOGIES. DIDN'T GET THE NEW GENDER-NEUTRAL *HANDBOOK* YET.

MAY I BORROW YOU FOR A MOMENT?

AM I ABOUT TO GET SPANKED, MARTY?

DEPENDS.

BECAUSE I USUALLY LEAVE THAT TO MY HUSBAND...

JENNIFER, I HOPE OUR PARTY IS GOING TO HAVE YOUR SUPPORT AGAINST THE AMENDMENT TO 1646.

OH, REALLY? AND SINCE WHEN DOES A MIGHTY SENATOR CARE ABOUT WHAT GOES ON IN THE LOWLY HOUSE?

DON'T BE CUTE, *CONGRESS-WOMAN.* NOW WILL WE HAVE YOUR VOTE OR NOT?

NO. YOU KNOW FULL WELL THAT I DON'T BELIEVE THE STATE DEPARTMENT SHOULD BE PROVIDING FOREIGN AID TO ORGANIZATIONS THAT PERFORM *ABORTIONS.*

I SEE. SO YOU DON'T THINK MEXICAN WOMEN SHOULD BE ALLOWED TO PLAN THE NUMBER OF CHILDREN THEY'LL HAVE?

OH, *PLEASE,* MARTY. ABORTION ISN'T A *CONTRACEPTIVE.* I JUST THINK THAT MONEY WOULD BE BETTER SPENT EDUCATING THE WORLD ABOUT ADVANCES LIKE THE MORNING-AFTER PILL.

THAT'S WHAT I WAS AFRAID OF. THIS IS A FUCKING *PRO-LIFE* THING, ISN'T IT?

JESUS, JENNIFER, WHAT KIND OF WOMAN *ARE* YOU?

THE SAME KIND OF WOMAN *YOU* ARE, MARTY. A DEMOCRAT.

BUT YOU'RE GOING TO SIDE WITH THE *GOP* ON THIS ONE.

YES...LIKE YOU DO 89% OF THE TIME ON *GUN CONTROL.*

WELL, THANKS FOR YOUR TIME THEN. I HOPE YOU ENJOY WHAT'S LEFT OF YOUR TERM.

IS THAT A *THREAT*, SENATOR?

I DON'T NEED TO THREATEN YOU, JEN.

YOU GOT LUCKY ONCE, BUT YOU WON'T GET ELECTED AGAIN ...NOT WITHOUT MY HELP.

EXCUSE ME, SIR. YOU'RE NEEDED IN THE WEST WING.

MY MEETING ISN'T UNTIL SEVEN.

THIS IS AT THE REQUEST OF *POTUS*, SIR. I WAS TOLD TO TELL YOU THAT IT CONCERNS *"355."*

WE'LL CONTINUE THIS DISCUSSION LATER, REPRESENTATIVE.

WHAT'S 355, MA'AM? THAT'S NOT A BILL, IS IT?

WHO KNOWS?

BUT IF HE'S MEETING WITH THE PRESIDENT, IT'S PROBABLY ABOUT *BASEBALL...*

SORRY, THAT WAS MOMMY DEAREST, BUSY BRINGING SHAME TO OHIO'S 22ND DISTRICT.

ANYWAY, HOW'S LIFE DOWN UNDER?

FUCKING *INCREDIBLE.* I WISH I COULD STAY OUT HERE ANOTHER MONTH... NO OFFENSE, OF COURSE.

YESTERDAY, THIS BIG-TIME ANTHROPOLOGIST TOOK US ON A TOUR OF THE DHARAWAL PEOPLE'S ANCIENT ROCK DWELLINGS AND SHOWED ME--

GODDAMN IT, AMPERSAND! STOP IT!

WHAT THE HELL IS AN AMPERSAND?

YOU KNOW, IT'S THAT CURLY SYMBOL FOR "AND," LIKE IN *TURNER & HOOCH* OR *TANGO & CASH*--

I KNOW WHAT AN AMPERSAND IS, ASSHEAD! WHY ARE YOU TALKING TO ONE?

BECAUSE HE'S THROWING HIS OWN SHIT AT ME!

OH, GOOD LORD. PLEASE DON'T TELL ME YOU BOUGHT A *CHIMP*...

I DIDN'T. HE'S A *MONKEY.* AND I DIDN'T *BUY* HIM, I *APPLIED* FOR HIM.

GET AWAY FROM MY WALLET, YOU *BASTARD!*

A GROUP IN BOSTON WAS LOOKING FOR PEOPLE TO TRAIN THE THINGS, SO I VOLUNTEERED.

THESE *FUCKERS* ARE SUPPOSED TO HELP QUADRIPLEGICS WITH THEIR DAILY CHORES AND SHIT... BUT DON'T ASK ME *HOW.*

WELL, YOU'VE ALREADY TAUGHT *YOUR* MONKEY TO FASTEN THE STRAPS OF A *STRAIGHTJACKET,* RIGHT?

HOW DID YOU...? I MEAN...

YOU WERE ON SPEAKERPHONE BEFORE... WHICH YOU ONLY DO DURING YOUR "AMAZING YORICK" ROUTINE... WHICH YOU ONLY DO WHEN YOU'RE *NERVOUS.*

I WAS PRETTY SURE YOU WERE HIDING *SOMETHING,* I JUST DIDN'T THINK IT WAS A *LIVING CREATURE!*

NOT BAD, SCULLY... BUT YOU'RE ONLY *HALF* RIGHT. IF YOU MUST KNOW, I *HAVE* BEEN A LITTLE NERVOUS ABOUT SOMETHING, BUT IT'S NOT...

AMPERSAND, TURN THAT *OFF!*

--PORTING FROM *THE WEST BANK,* I'M CHRISTOPHER EMANUEL...

Nablus, West Bank
Eighteen Minutes Ago

HEY!

YEAH, *YOU*, PRIVATE BENJAMIN! THEY'RE JUST *KIDS!* WHAT THE HELL ARE YOU *DOING?*

I AM FIRING RUBBER BULLETS. AS WARNING SHOTS. WELL ABOVE THE PALESTINIANS' HEADS.

AND MY NAME IS *COLONEL* TSE'ELON. IF YOU EVER AGAIN REFER TO ME AS PRIVATE *ANY-THING,* I WILL NOT AFFORD *YOU!* SUCH COURTESY.

OH, MY... MY BAD. *HEH.*

I'M CHRISTOPHER, BY THE WAY. HOW WOULD YOU LIKE TO BE ON *TV?* I'M SUPPOSED TO DO A PIECE ABOUT FEMALE COMBAT SOLDIERS WHILE I'M OUT HERE.

YOU KNOW, SEE HOW YOU LADIES FEEL ABOUT THE *IDF* ABOLISH-ING THE WOMEN'S CORPS ...FIND OUT WHAT IT'S LIKE TO FIGHT ALONG-SIDE THE BOYS AS EQUA--

YOU HAVE TO LEAVE. NOW. NONE OF YOU ARE SAFE HERE.

DARLING, WE WORK FOR ONE OF THE TOP *SIX* CABLE NEWS ORGANIZATIONS IN AMERICA. WE DON'T *HAVE* TO DO ANY-THING.

BUT WE WILL *VOLUNTEER* TO BE ESCORTED OUT... *IF* YOU LET ME INTERVIEW YOU ALONG THE WAY. I'LL EVEN PROMISE NOT TO--

WHATEVER. COME.

BO'U NELEKH!

SO, UH, YOU HAVE A *FIRST* NAME, COLONEL?

YES...

...BUT I DO NOT KNOW WHAT IT IS.

KEEP YOUR HEADS DOWN...

TWO OF MY SIBLINGS DIED AT BIRTH, SO WHEN MY PARENTS HAD ME, THEY DECIDED NOT TO SPEAK MY NAME OUT LOUD.

IT IS A STUPID OLD TRADITION, DONE TO "DECEIVE THE ANGEL OF DEATH," CONFUSE HIM SO THAT HE WILL NOT KNOW WHERE TO FIND ME.

BUT... WHAT DO YOUR *FRIENDS* CALL YOU?

ALTER.

A NICKNAME. MEANS "OLD ONE." IT IS A...LONG STORY.

AREN'T MOM AND POP WORRIED ABOUT THE ANGEL OF DEATH FINDING YOU OUT *HERE*?

THEY NEED NOT BE CONCERNED. I HAVE YET TO BE FIRED UPON.

YOU ALMOST SOUND *DISAPPOINTED.*

OF COURSE. JOINING AN ARTILLERY BATTALION HAS ALWAYS BEEN MY DREAM, BUT NOW THAT I AM FINALLY PERMITTED TO BE A PART OF ONE...WE ENCOUNTER NOTHING BUT *STONE-THROWERS.*

MAN, YOU ARE *HARDCORE.* EVERY OTHER DAUGHTER OF ISRAEL I TALK TO OUT HERE IS JUST HAPPY THAT IT'S ALL QUIET ON THE WESTERN FRONT.

THOSE GIRLS COULD BE PARATROOPERS OR NAVAL COMMANDERS... BUT MEN HAVE TAUGHT THEM TO BE CONTENT BEHIND A TYPEWRITER OR RADAR SCREEN. NOT ME.

MY GRANDMOTHER CROSSED INTO ENEMY LINES DURING OUR WAR OF INDEPENDENCE, AND *HER* GRANDMOTHER WAS PART OF THE ALL-FEMALE BATTALION OF DEATH DURING THE RUSSIAN REVOLUTION.

THIS IS WHO I *AM*...

I DON'T GET IT. I MEAN, *OFF THE RECORD,* I UNDERSTAND FIGHTING FOR EQUAL PAY AND ALL THAT GARBAGE... BUT I THOUGHT YOU FEMINISTS WERE *PACIFISTS,* TOO.

WHO WANTS PEACE...

...WHEN WE HAVE NOT YET BEGUN TO FIGHT?

YORICK, YOU ARE A *MENTAL PATIENT!*

YOU COULDN'T KEEP *SEA MONKEYS* ALIVE, REMEMBER? WHY IN THE WORLD WOULD YOU GET A *REAL* ONE?

I DON'T KNOW... I GUESS I JUST WANTED TO DO SOMETHING *PRODUCTIVE* WITH MY ABUNDANT "FREE TIME."

I MEAN, YOU AND THE REST OF MY GLOBETROTTING FRIENDS ARE ALL OFF SAVING THE WORLD OR WHATEVER, BUT I HAVEN'T DONE A GODDAMN THING FOR *ANYONE.*

SO WHY DON'T YOU SPEND A SUMMER WITH HABITAT FOR HUMANITY... OR SIGN UP WITH THE PEACE CORPS?

WELL, I KNOW THIS SOUNDS RETARDED, BUT SINCE YOU LEFT, I THINK I'VE BECOME TOTALLY *AGORAPHOBIC.*

I USED TO LOVE TO GO OUT, BUT I'M GROWING UNCOMFORTABLY... *COMFORTABLE* IN THIS DUNGEON. SOME DAYS, I CAN'T EVEN GET PAST THE FRONT DOOR.

I'M THE ESCAPE ARTIST WHO CAN'T ESCAPE HIS APARTMENT.

THAT'S CRAZY, COUNTRY MOUSE!

THE WORLD IS A GLORIOUS PLACE. WHAT'S THERE TO BE AFRAID OF...?

SHH...

Al Karak, Jordan
Thirteen Minutes Ago

DR. FROZAN HAMAD?

WHO ARE YOU? HOW DID YOU FIND ME?

THERE'S NO TIME FOR THAT, MA'AM.

MA'AM? YOU'RE... YOU'RE *AMERICAN*. WHY WOULD *YOU* WANT TO KILL ME?

I DON'T.

I'M HERE TO HELP YOU ESCAPE.

WHAT THE HELL ARE YOU TALKING ABOUT?

THIS IS MY *HOME*.

TELL THE UNITED NATIONS OR...OR *WHO-EVER* SENT YOU THAT I HAVE NO NEED FOR THEIR POLITICAL ASYLUM. JORDAN IS FAR FROM PERFECT, BUT WE'RE NOT *SAUDI ARABIA*.

DOCTOR, YOU'VE BEEN IN HIDING FOR *MONTHS*. HOW MANY MORE ASSASSINATION ATTEMPTS DO YOU THINK YOU CAN SURVIVE?

AS MANY AS IT TAKES. I REFUSE TO LET A HANDFUL OF MUSLIM *EXTREMISTS* DERAIL MY EFFORTS TO END THE "HONOR KILLING" OF MY SISTERS.

THAT'S NOT WHAT THIS IS ABOUT.

OH, NO?

ONE FOURTH OF THE MURDERS COMMITTED IN MY COUNTRY ARE WOMEN KILLED BY MALE RELATIVES WHO SIMPLY *ACCUSE* THEM OF ADULTERY OR...OR "FORNICATION".

OUR PENAL CODE *SANCTIONS* THOSE CRIMES BY GRANTING LESSER SENTENCES, IF *ANY* SENTENCES, TO THE MON-STERS W...

YOU DON'T UNDERSTAND, FROZAN.

THE MEN WHO'VE MADE ATTEMPTS ON YOUR LIFE AREN'T INTERESTED IN YOUR POLITICS.

THEY'RE INTERESTED IN WHAT'S AROUND YOUR NECK.

I...I DON'T FOLLOW.

THEY'RE AFTER THE AMULET OF HELENE, DOCTOR.

AMULET?

IT'S A WORTHLESS NECKLACE, A... A CRUDE STONE IDOL!

THEN YOU'LL PART WITH IT? BEFORE SOMEONE GETS HURT?

NEVER.

MY FATHER TOLD ME THAT A CATASTROPHE COMPARABLE TO THE *TROJAN WAR* WOULD TAKE PLACE IF IT WERE EVER REMOVED FROM THIS LAND.

AND YOU *BELIEVE* THAT?

OF COURSE NOT... BUT I DO BELIEVE IN *TRADITION*. THIS ARTIFACT HAS BEEN IN MY FAMILY FOR GENERATIONS, AND I HAVE NO INTENTION OF GIVING IT OVER TO ANYONE... CERTAINLY NOT AN *ARMED INTRUDER*.

WHAT *IS* YOUR INTEREST IN ALL OF THIS? WHO ARE YOU WORKING FOR?

I'LL EXPLAIN ON THE WAY TO THE AIRSTRIP.

YOU'RE NOT SAFE HERE, FROZAN. IF *I* WAS ABLE TO FIND YOU, SO WILL...

BLAM! BLAM! BLAM!

RAHHHH!

FUCK!

HNF

DAMN IT!

GODDAMN IT!

CULPER RING, THIS ...THIS IS AGENT 355.

INFORM THE PRESIDENT THERE'S GOING TO BE A... A SLIGHT DELAY.

I'M NOT AFRAID OF THE WORLD...

...I'M AFRAID OF A WORLD WITHOUT *YOU.*

OH, BROTHER.

I THINK YOU WERE HANGING UPSIDE-DOWN A LITTLE TOO LONG, BABE.

I MEAN IT, BETH. I REALLY FEEL LOST WHEN WE'RE APART.

I KNOW. I'VE MISSED YOU TOO, YORICK.

I WAS JUST THINKING ABOUT THAT TIME WE WERE ON YOUR ROOF, IN THE *RAIN...*

BUT IT'S NOT JUST THAT! I MEAN, OF *COURSE* I MISS THAT, BUT...

YOU'RE MY BEST FRIEND, BETH. YOU'RE BRILLIANT AND FUNNY AND YOUR FAVORITE MOVIE IS *MILLER'S CROSSING.* I DIDN'T EVEN KNOW THERE *WERE* WOMEN LIKE YOU.

YOU MAKE ME A BETTER, SMARTER, *BRAVER* PERSON, AND I DON'T WANT TO

YORICK, WAIT.

BEFORE YOU SAY ANYTHING, THERE'S... THERE'S SOMETHING I SHOULD TELL YOU.

Boston, Massachusetts
Seven Minutes Ago

NO WORRIES, DOC. PROBABLY JUST BRAXTON HICKS CONTRACTIONS.

I ASSURE YOU, THIS IS *TRUE LABOR*.

WELL, WE'LL SEE. WHO'S YOUR DOCTOR?

I DON'T HAVE ONE.

WHAT?

YOU'RE IN YOUR THIRD TRIMESTER AND YOU HAVEN'T *SEEN* SOME- ONE YET?

MICHAEL, *PLEASE.*

A LITTLE DOCTOR-PATIENT CONFIDENTIALITY...?

SUNIL HAS BEEN PROVIDING PRENATAL CARE AND PERFORMING APPROPRIATE TESTS.

IS...IS HE THE FATHER?

NO, HE'S MY RESEARCH ASSISTANT.

I'M THE FATHER.

I...I DON'T UNDER-STAND...

YOU'RE A...

JESUS CHRIST. YOU'RE *JOKING*, RIGHT? YOU'RE...YOU'RE NOT SERIOUSLY HAVING YOUR OWN *CLONE?*

YES. I AM.

BUT...HOW? *WHY?*

WOULD IT BE POSSIBLE FOR ME TO *EHN* EXPLAIN THAT *AFTER* YOU'VE DELIVERED THE BABY?

I CAN'T. I MEAN...IF YOU'RE TELLING THE TRUTH, THIS PROBABLY ISN'T EVEN *LEGAL*.

THEN YOU CAN CONCERN YOURSELF WITH ALERTING THE PROPER AUTHORITIES...OR YOU CAN HELP SAVE THIS CHILD'S LIFE.

FINE.

BUT WE CAN'T DO THIS HERE...

Boston, Massachusetts
Four Minutes Ago

YO, JOE! YOU IN THERE?

SHOWTIME, HERO!

WELL, IF THE PROFESSOR WANTED KIDS WHO LOVED HIM, HE SHOULDN'T HAVE GIVEN US SUCH STUPID NAMES...YES, I'M KIDDING! GOOD-BYE, MOTHER!

PUT YOUR PANTS ON, BRO! DIDN'T YOU HEAR THE FUCKIN' ALARM? WE GOT A GETAWAY DOWN BY THE HARBOR.

THANK CHRIST. BEEN AGES SINCE WE HAD ANYTHING BUT *BOMB THREATS* AROUND HERE.

OH, HEY, BROWN, SORRY TO INTERRUPT THE CONJUGAL. MIND IF I STEAL YOUR MAN FOR A JOB?

NO WORRIES, LARRY. YOU NEED MY TEAM?

NOT YET, COUNTY'S ALREADY ON THE SCENE. BIG-ASS CHEMICAL FIRE, BUT IT SOUNDS LIKE THEY'VE GOT EVERYBODY OUT OF THE PLANT.

WHAT...A... *WHOREBAG.*

HAS "ZERO" EFFED *EVERY* FIREFIGHTER FROM LAST YEAR'S CALENDAR NOW?

PROBABLY. BUT SHE SWEARS THIS GUY'S "THE ONE." I HOPE HE GIVES HER HERPES...

YOU BE CAREFUL OF THOSE FUMES, PRETTY BOY.

AND YOU KEEP THAT BUS WARM FOR ME. I'LL BE BACK IN A FLASH.

OH, POOR CHOICE OF WORDS. I JUST COME BACK *SAFE,* OKAY, JOE?

DON'T!

PLEASE. I KNOW YOU HATE IT WHEN I GET ALL SERIOUS, BUT JUST LET ME SAY THIS ONE THING. IT'S IMPORTANT...

I LIED TO YOU, BETH.

YOU DID?

ABOUT WHAT?

I DIDN'T GIVE HALF OF MY CASH TO A CORRUPT COP IN THE PARK.

I SPENT IT.

ON...ON WHAT?

NOTHING EXTRAVAGANT, JUST A LITTLE TRINKET I FOUND IN THAT MAGIC STORE I GO TO...BUT IT'S WHAT I'VE BEEN SO NERVOUS ABOUT.

LISTEN, I KNOW THIS IS UNBELIEVABLY TACKY TO DO OVER THE PHONE, BUT I KEEP HAVING NIGHTMARES ABOUT YOU BEING EATEN BY DINGOES BEFORE I CAN ASK...

SO HERE GOES EVERY-THING...

Brooklyn, New York Five Seconds Ago

BETH DEVILLE... WILL YOU MARRY ME?

Washington, D.C. Four Seconds Ago

REPRESENTATIVE BROWN? YOUR HUSBAND JUST CALLED. HE'S GOING TO BE LATE FOR HIS PARTY TONIGHT.

MEN. CAN'T LIVE *WITH* 'EM...

Nablus, West Bank Three Seconds Ago

SO, uh, WHAT TIME DOES YOUR PATROL END?

QUIET. DID YOU HEAR THAT?

SOUNDED LIKE *SHELLING*...

20,000 Feet Above Jordan Two Seconds Ago

THREE BODIES FOR ONE RECOVERED ARTIFACT, HUH, 355? YOU'RE TURNING INTO THE CULPER RING'S LARA CROF

JUST SHUT UP AND GET US OUT OF HERE, 1033.

TAKE IT EASY, WE'RE ABOUT TO HIT SAUDI AIRSPACE...

Boston, Massachusetts One Second Ago

THIS...THIS ISN'T RIGHT.

NOW

Tokyo Stock
Exchange, Japan

St. Peters,
Vatican City

King Hill, Idaho

DADDY?
I THINK BUCK
IS *SICK*...

Amsterdam,
the Netherlands

VIDEOS

São Paulo, Brazil

Johnson Space Center, Texas

MISSION CONTROL

ENVIORMENTAL

HOUSTON, HOUSTON, DO YOU READ?

Leningrad Nuclear Power Plant, Russia

BEEP EEP EEP EEP-EPP EEP EEP EEP EEP

Mombasa, Kenya

Washington, D.C.
Two Months Later

HHHNNNNNNNNNNNNNNNNNNNNNNNNNN

OUCH.

OH MY GOD!

LADY, ARE YOU *OKAY*?

YEAH, I... I'M FINE.

YOU SURE? WHAT'S WRONG WITH YOUR *VOICE?*

JUST... GOT THE *WIND* KNOCKED OUT OF ME...

I AM *SO* SORRY.

I JUST STARTED DRIVING THIS THING AND I STILL *SUCK* AT BRAKING. DOESN'T EXACTLY HANDLE LIKE MY OLD *MIATA,* YOU KNOW?

IF YOU HADN'T BEEN ALL LUCY LAWLESS BACK THERE, I PROBABLY WOULD'VE...

AW, *SHIT!*

WHAT IS IT...?

UNMANNED CHAPTER TWO

BRIAN K. VAUGHAN * PIA GUERRA
WRITER/CO-CREATORS/ARTIST

JOSE MARZAN, Jr. inker **CLEM ROBINS** letterer **PAM RAMBO** colorist
DIGITAL CHAMELEON separations **J.G. JONES** cover artist
ZACHARY RAU assistant editor **HEIDI MacDONALD** editor

THEY FELL OUT.

OH, CHRIST, THEY'RE ALL...

ALL *MINE*, YEP.

BUT IF YOU GIMME A QUICK HAND THROWING THESE DUDES BACK IN THE TRUCK... I MIGHT *CONSIDER* SHARING THE PROFITS.

THIS... THIS IS YOUR *JOB*?

BELIEVE IT OR NOT. TURNS OUT THERE'S STILL A *TON* OF SINGLE GUYS ROTTING IN THEIR APARTMENTS AND STINKING UP OFFICE BUILDINGS.

EVERYONE'S WORRIED ABOUT DISEASES AND SHIT, SO THE *CDC* GIVES ME A CAN OF FOOD FOR EVERY CORPSE I BRING IN. ONLY WORK I COULD FIND...

FUCKED UP, HUH? I USED TO HAVE A MODELING CONTRACT WITH *WILHELMINA*, AND NOW I'M A GODDAMN *GARBAGE* GIRL.

WORST PART IS, I SPENT *THREE GRAND* ON MY BOOB JOB JUST BEFORE EVERYTHING HAPPENED. FAT LOT OF GOOD OUR TITS DO US NOW, RIGHT?

WHAT... WHAT DO YOU *DO* WITH THESE BODIES?

I TAKE 'EM OVER TO *RFK*.

THEY TURNED THE STADIUM INTO ONE OF THOSE, WHATCHAMACALLITS ...*CREMATORIUMS*.

YOU ALL RIGHT? JUST TAKE A FEW DEEP BREATHS.

YOU DON'T HAVE TO WEAR THAT *MASK* ANYMORE, YOU KNOW. IF WHATEVER WIPED *THEM* OUT COULD'VE KILLED *US* ...WE'D BE DEAD *ALREADY*.

YEAH, WELL, BETTER SAFE THAN SORRY...

WHERE DID YOU GET *THAT*?

THIS? TOOK IT OFF A DEAD COP LAST MONTH.

I GOT IT AFTER MY BOYFRIEND WAS MURDERED.

WAIT, DID YOU SAY...?

YEAH, SHE WAS A *TRANNY*, FEMALE TO MALE. WE MET AT ONE OF THE FUNERALS.

BUT I GUESS THE AMAZONS THOUGHT SHE WAS A *REAL* GUY, 'CAUSE THEY KILLED HER THE SECOND THEY SAW HER.

AMAZONS?

ARE... ARE THOSE THE GANGS THAT HAVE BEEN BURNING DOWN ALL THE *SPERM BANKS*?

HADN'T HEARD THAT ONE. PROBABLY.

THOSE BITCHES ARE *PSYCHO*. THEY THINK *GOD* WANTED ALL THE MEN DEAD. I MEAN, EVERY-BODY KNOWS THE *ARABS* DID IT.

WELL, NO ONE KNOWS FOR *SURE* WHAT--

HEY, WHAT'S IN THE CARRIER?

YOU GOT A CAT OR A DOG?

AH, *PLEASE* DON'T TOUCH THAT...

TAKE IT EASY, I'M NOT GONNA *EAT* HER. I *LOVE* ANIMALS.

I USED TO HAVE THESE THREE PUPPIES, FRANK, DEAN, AND SAMMY? BUT THEY ALL DIED. YOU'RE SO LUCKY YOU'VE GOT A GIRL...

...MONKEY?

DAMMIT, AMPERSAND!

STOP IT! GET THE HELL OFF MY--

... HI THERE.

Alexandria, Virginia
Earlier Today

IF YOU'RE LOOKING FOR FOOD, THE KITCHEN'S ALREADY BEEN *PILLAGED*.

MARGARET VALENTINE?

THANK GOD YOU'RE SAFE. I WAS AFRAID YOU'D BEEN KIDNAPPED.

HOW...HOW DID YOU KNOW MY NAME? THIS ISN'T EVEN MY *HOUSE*.

MS. VALENTINE, I'M AGENT 355. I WORK FOR A...*COVERT* ARM OF THE EXECUTIVE BRANCH CALLED THE CULPER RING. I'M HERE TO ESCORT YOU BACK TO WASHINGTON.

WHY...? I'M THE SECRETARY OF *AGRI-CULTURE*. MOST OF THE FARMERS AND LIVESTOCK ARE *DEAD*.

ACTUALLY, YOUR TITLE HAS *CHANGED*.

OH, REALLY? WHAT AM I NOW... SECRETARY OF HOPELESS CAUSES?

NO, MA'AM...

YOU'RE PRESIDENT OF THE UNITED STATES.

WHAT ARE YOU *TALKING* ABOUT?

THEY WERE ALL MEN, MA'AM.

VICE PRESIDENT, SPEAKER OF THE HOUSE, PRESIDENT PRO TEMPORE OF THE SENATE, SECRETARIES OF STATE, TREASURY, AND DEFENSE...

...AND THE ATTORNEY GENERAL, TOO. YES, I *UNDERSTAND* THE CHAIN OF SUCCESSION.

BUT THERE ARE CABINET POSITIONS *AHEAD* OF ME! WHAT ABOUT OUR...OUR SECRETARY OF THE *INTERIOR*? THE CONSTITUTION SAYS *SHE'S* NEXT IN LINE!

I'M AFRAID SECRETARY RICHBURG DIED IN ONE OF THE CRASHES, MADAM PRESIDENT.

JESUS, DON'T *CALL* ME THAT!

YOU CAN'T KEEP HIDING, MA'AM, YOU'RE THE HIGHEST-RANKING WOMAN IN AMERICA NOW... AND YOUR GOVERNMENT DOESN'T EVEN KNOW YOU'RE *ALIVE*.

GOOD! I'M JUST A...A *STUPID* FARM GIRL WHO MISSES HER WORTHLESS EX-HUSBAND. I'M NOT *QUALIFIED* TO BE PRESIDENT!

YES, MARGARET. YOU *ARE*.

I KNOW MORE ABOUT YOU THAN YOU MIGHT THINK. I TRAVELED A A LONG, *LONG* WAY TO FIND YOU BECAUSE I *BELIEVE* IN YOU. I BELIEVE YOU'RE THE LEADER WE *NEED* RIGHT NOW.

WHEN YOU TOOK YOUR OATH, YOU SWORE TO BE A *STEWARD* OF THIS LAND.

ARE YOU STILL WILLING TO SERVE?

NO FUCKING WAY!

WHO ARE YOU?

MY NAME'S YORICK.

HOW DID YOU...?

I DON'T KNOW.

PLEASE, I'M JUST TRYING TO FIND MY--

HEY!

uh, WHAT...WHAT ARE YOU...?

I DON'T BELIEVE IT.

YOU'RE A REAL MAN...

...BUT JUST BARELY.

OH, THANKS A *LOT*.

HANDLING ROTTING *CORPSES* TENDS TO GIVE ME A BIT OF *SHRINKAGE*, OKAY? YOU CAN'T EXPECT A GUY TO--

GET INSIDE THE TRUCK.

WHAT?

WHAT ARE YOU GOING TO DO, *RAPE* ME?

DON'T FLATTER YOURSELF.

YOU'RE NOT MY *TYPE*.

OH.

THEN... WHAT *ARE* YOU GONNA DO?

I'M GOING TO SELL YOU.

HOLD ON, SELL ME TO **WHOM?**

"WHOM"?

WHAT ARE YOU, AN ENGLISH MAJOR?

WASTE DISPOSAL

AS A MATTER OF FACT--

YEAH, I REALLY DON'T CARE.

NO OFFENSE, BUT I HAVEN'T EATEN IN A **WEEK,** AND THERE'S A GROUP IN HAGERSTOWN THAT WILL PROBABLY PAY ENOUGH FOOD TO LAST THE REST OF MY **LIFE** FOR YOU.

DON'T WORRY, I'LL TAKE YOU THERE AS SOON AS I FINISH LOADING THE REST OF THESE BOYS!

I MEAN, IF **YOU** SURVIVED, THERE ARE PROBABLY **OTHER** GUYS ALIVE OUT THERE!

I WANT TO TRADE YOU IN WHILE YOU'RE STILL AN **EXCLUSIVE,** BEFORE SOME OTHER MAN MYSTERIOUSLY...

...APPEARS?

IF THOSE HAD BEEN *DARBY* CUFFS, THAT CHICK WOULD PROBABLY BE SELLING US TO SOME *BROTHEL* RIGHT ABOUT NOW.

CHEEP CAW

NO, THEY *WOULDN'T* HAVE FED US. THEY WOULD HAVE FED *ME*. YOU, THEY WOULD HAVE *BARBECUED*.

YOU'RE JUST LUCKY THOSE HANDCUFFS WERE *HIATTS*, YOU LITTLE SHIT.

AW SEEK SEEK

WHATEVER, DUDE. I'M STARVING, TOO.

OBVIOUSLY, SINCE I'M HAVING A FUCKING CONVERSATION WITH A *MONKEY*.

BUT GRUB HAS TO WAIT...

...UNTIL WE'VE FOUND MY MOM.

REPRESENTATIVE BROWN?

JESUS, DIANE!

I CAME *THIS* CLOSE TO ASSAULTING YOU WITH THREE YEARS' WORTH OF *TAE BO* CLASSES.

EXIT

SORRY, MA'AM. DIDN'T MEAN TO STARTLE YOU, JUST DOING MY LAST SECURITY SWEEP OF THE NIGHT.

WOULD YOU LIKE ME TO ESCORT YOU HOME NOW?

NO. THANK YOU.

I...I THINK I'M GOING TO STAY HERE TONIGHT. THE OTHER MEMBERS OF CONGRESS AND I ARE STILL TRYING TO DECIDE ON A NEW COMMANDER IN CHIEF FOR YOU LADIES TO PROTECT.

JEN, YOU HAVEN'T LEFT THE WHITE HOUSE IN *THREE DAYS*.

WELL, CAN YOU BLAME ME? EVEN WITHOUT ELECTRICITY, THIS PLACE IS STILL A *PALACE* COMPARED TO MY OLD RAYBURN OFFICE.

IT'S OKAY, DIANE. *HONESTLY*, GO HOME TO YOUR... TO YOUR GIRLS.

YOU POSITIVE?

SPECIAL AGENT FERRIS IS IN CHARGE OF THE WEST WING TONIGHT. IF YOU NEED *ANYTHING*...

GOOD *NIGHT*, DIANE.

I PRAYED EVERY SECOND, YORICK.

I PRAYED EVERY SECOND FOR YOU. BUT I NEVER THOUGHT--

I'M SO SORRY. IT TOOK ME WEEKS TO GET OUT OF NEW YORK.

ARE YOU...?

THE ONLY ONE?

I DON'T KNOW. I THINK SO. UNLESS DAD...

I MEAN, IS DADDY STILL...?

DAMN.

DAMN.

DAMN!

DAMN!

I...I THOUGHT MAYBE IT WAS GENETIC.

I THOUGHT THAT WHATEVER KEPT ME ALIVE MIGHT HAVE...

I...I...

I DIDN'T CALL HIM.

IT WAS HIS BIRTHDAY AND I DIDN'T CALL HIM.

HONEY BOY...

HERO?

WHAT ABOUT HERO?

NO, I...

I WAS HOPING *YOU'D* HEARD FROM YOUR SISTER.

UH-UH. PHONES ARE DOWN ALL OVER. BUT...BUT I'M SURE SHE'S OKAY, MOM. SHE'S PROBABLY--

WHAT THE HELL IS *THAT?!*

OH...SORRY. THIS IS AMPERSAND. I STARTED TRAINING HIM AFTER YOU TOLD ME TO DO MORE VOLUNTEER WORK. HE'S A HELPER MONKEY. SUPPOSEDLY...

"HE"? BUT... I THOUGHT EVERY MAMMAL WITH A Y CHROMOSOME WAS...

YORICK, *HOW?* HOW DID YOU...?

I HAVE NO IDEA. ALL OF THE *OTHER* MEN IN MY BUILDING DIED. ALL OF MY MALE *FRIENDS* DIED. EVERY GUY I *KNOW* DIED. I DON'T GET IT...

...BUT I THINK IT MIGHT HAVE SOMETHING TO DO WITH THIS *RING.*

I BOUGHT IT IN A MAGIC STORE AND USED IT TO PROPOSE TO BETH RIGHT BEFORE--

A MAGIC *RING?* YORICK, DON'T BE *RIDICULOUS,* THAT HAS NOTHING TO DO WITH...

DID YOU SAY YOU *PROPOSED?*

WELL... WHAT DID SHE *SAY*?

"YES."

AT LEAST, I *THINK* SHE DID. WE SORTA GOT DISCONNECTED BEFORE I COULD HEAR HER ANSWER.

THAT'S WHY I'M GOING TO *AUSTRALIA*... TO FIND OUT FOR SURE.

THE *HELL* YOU ARE!

YORICK BROWN, YOU MAY VERY WELL BE THE LAST MAN ON EARTH! YOU HAVE A RESPONSIBILITY TO THE *WORLD* NOW!

WHAT, TO REPOPULATE THE *PLANET* FOR YOU?

LISTEN, I *WANT* TO HELP, MOM. I REALLY DO. THAT'S WHY I CAME TO YOU FIRST.

BUT I DON'T WANT TO SIT HERE AND BE A..."STUD" FOR HOWEVER MANY ANONYMOUS WOMEN YOU EXPECT ME TO *INSEMINATE*.

NOT WHEN THE GIRL I *LOVE* IS OUT THERE.

YORICK, I HAVE NO INTENTION OF WHORING OUT MY OWN *SON*.

I JUST THINK THAT YOU HAVE MORE IMPORTANT THINGS TO DO THAN ENGAGE IN SOME KIND OF ROMANTIC *CRUSADE*.

LIKE *WHAT*?

OH, I DON'T KNOW... PREVENTING THE EXTINCTION OF THE *HUMAN RACE*?

THAT'S WHAT I'M *PLANNING* TO DO!

WITH *BETH*.

SWEETIE, ADAM AND EVE TO THE CONTRARY, YOU CAN'T DO THAT WITH JUST *TWO PEOPLE*.

YEAH.

YEAH, I *KNOW*... BUT WHAT AM I *SUPPOSED* TO DO, MOM?

I'M NOT SURE...BUT *SHE* MIGHT BE ABLE TO TELL YOU.

HER NAME'S DR. ALISON MANN, BIOENGINEER OUT OF BOSTON. SUPPOSEDLY, SHE KNOWS MORE ABOUT ASEXUAL REPRODUCTION THAN ANYONE ALIVE.

WE WERE HOPING THAT SHE'D HELP US CREATE THE NEXT GENERATION OF *FEMALES*, BUT IF SHE COULD FIND OUT WHAT MAKES *YOU* IMMUNE--

WAIT A SECOND... YOU MEAN *CLONING*? I THOUGHT YOU HELPED *OUTLAW* THAT.

I DID.

BUT THIS ISN'T THE SAME WORLD IT WAS TWO MONTHS AGO.

WELL, *THAT'S* THE UNDERSTATEMENT OF THE--

Interstate 395, Virginia
Six Hours Ago

WHAT'S THE MATTER? WHY'D WE STOP?

I'M AFRAID WE'RE GOING TO HAVE TO WALK THE REST OF THE WAY, MADAM PRESIDENT.

I THOUGHT I TOLD YOU TO STOP CALLING ME...

DID YOU SAY WALK?

ARE YOU OUT OF YOUR MIND, AGENT 395? WE'RE IN THE MIDDLE OF I-355! THE WHITE HOUSE IS MILES FROM HERE!

I BEG YOUR PARDON, MA'AM, BUT IT'S INTERSTATE 395 AND AGENT 355.

WHAT DO I LOOK LIKE, A NUMEROLOGIST?

ALL I'M SAYING IS, IF THAT CAR WAS OUT OF GAS, WE CAN JUST GRAB ANOTHER. IT'S NOT LIKE THERE'S A SHORTAGE.

WE'LL FIND A NEW VEHICLE WHEN WE REACH THE CITY, MA'AM.

BUT WHATEVER KILLED ALL THE MEN HAPPENED DURING RUSH HOUR...

The White House
Now

YOU SURE YOU'RE NOT JUMPING TO CONCLUSIONS, *REPRESENTATIVE?* I MEAN, NOT *EVERY* PERSON WHO OWNS A GUN IS A REPUBLICAN.

I *RECOGNIZE* THESE WOMEN, YORICK.

THEY'RE ALL WIVES OF *CONGRESS-MEN.*

LISTEN UP! THOSE WERE JUST *WARNING SHOTS!*

WE DON'T WANT TO HURT *ANYONE*...BUT WE CAN NO LONGER TOLERATE YOUR COUP OF OUR GOVERNMENT.

GRAB YOUR MONKEY.

WE'RE GETTING OUT OF HERE.

COUP? YOU MEAN...THEY WEREN'T SHOOTING AT *ME?*

THERE ARE ONLY THIRTEEN FEMALES IN THE SENATE AND SIXTY IN THE HOUSE ...AND ALMOST *THREE-FOURTHS* OF US ARE DEMOCRATS.

A FEW OF THE WIVES OF DEAD REPUBLICANS THINK WE'RE TRYING TO *ELIMINATE* THE TWO-PARTY SYSTEM JUST BECAUSE WE'RE NOT *GIVING* THEM THEIR HUSBANDS' SEATS.

ARE YOU *SERIOUS?* AFTER ALL THE MEN DIED, I THOUGHT YOU GUYS WOULD BE HOLDING HANDS DOWN AT THE UNITED NATIONS OR SOMETHING.

WHEN THE HELL DID WOMEN GET SO PETTY AND...AND *POWER-HUNGRY?*

DIDN'T YOU VOTE FOR *HILLARY?*

POINT.

ANYWAY, HOW ARE WE GONNA STOP THEM?

WE'RE NOT. YOU AND I ARE GOING TO A FALLOUT SHELTER UNDERNEATH THE EAST WING. EISENHOWER BUILT IT TO BE COMPLETELY IMPENETRABLE.

WHAT, YOU REALLY THINK A BUNCH OF FIFTY-SOMETHING *WIDOWS* CAN LAY SIEGE TO THE *WHITE HOUSE?*

WELL, *CANADIANS* NEARLY BURNT IT DOWN IN 1814... SO I SUPPOSE *ANYTHING'S* POSSIBLE.

YEAH, BUT THE CANUCKS HAD HELP FROM...

WOW, IS THAT A *DAYTON* TIME LOCK?

SECRET SERVICE ADDED IT DURING REAGAN'S FIRST TERM... TO MAKE SURE THAT RON DIDN'T ACCIDENTALLY STUMBLE OUT INTO A NUCLEAR WINTER, I GUESS.

ONCE THE DOOR IS CLOSED, IT'LL STAY SHUT FOR WHAT THEY THOUGHT WAS THE HALF-LIFE OF FALLOUT, THIRTY YEARS OR SO.

NO UNAUTHORIZED ACCESS

IT CAN ONLY BE OPENED PREMATURELY FROM THE *OUTSIDE* ... BY SOMEONE WITH PROPER SECURITY CLEARANCE.

THEN... WHO'S GOING TO GET US OUT?

NOT *US*, YORICK.

CLANG

HEY!

I'M SORRY, HONEY BOY.

BUT I COULDN'T RISK YOU DOING SOMETHING *STUPID* UP THERE.

OH, NO.

SHE'S GONNA DO SOMETHING *STUPID* UP THERE...

THERE YOU ARE!

SENATOR CAVANAUGH.

I...I DIDN'T KNOW YOU WERE STILL HERE.

DID YOU *SEE*, JENNIFER? THE G.O.P. IS STORMING THE *GODDAMN ROSE GARDEN*!

I GUESS WE'RE THE ONLY TWO POLITICOS WHO DIDN'T GO HOME FOR THE NIGHT. LUCKY US, HUH?

SECRET SERVICE WANTS US TO GET INSIDE THE OLD IKE BUNKER UNTIL THEY'VE--

NO!

I MEAN...WE CAN'T JUST STAY DOWN HERE AND *HIDE*.

WE SHOULD START A *DIALOGUE*, SENATOR. PUT A STOP TO THIS BEFORE SOMEONE ENDS UP *DEAD*.

OF...OF COURSE YOU'RE *RIGHT*.

WHAT THE HELL GOOD WOULD WE BE IN THERE?

SON OF A **BITCH**.

LITERALLY.

IF I DON'T STOP HER, MOM'S GONNA GET HERSELF **KILLED!**

AK OH OH

RIGHT, RELAX... WE'VE GOT A YALE LOCK ON THE INSIDE. THAT'S GOOD.

I MIGHT BE ABLE TO SHIM IT OPEN AND **REWIRE** THE DAYTON...

OKAY, GIMME SOME ROOM, AMPERSAND. THAT GOTH CHICK STOLE MY PICK KIT BACK IN JERSEY... SO I'M GONNA HAVE TO **REGURGITATE** THE TENSION TOOL I SWALLOWED.

HERE WE GO...

HHH...

...AHUH...

HWUHHH

HM.

THAT'S... THAT'S JUST THE FROZEN CHICKEN CUTLET I ATE FOR LUNCH.

OH, **GROSS!**

AMPERSAND, DON'T **EAT** THAT!

STEP AWAY FROM HER!

NOW!

DIANE! WHAT'S THE SITUATION?

I'M SORRY, MA'AM, BUT... BUT I WAS SO LOW ON STAFF AND OVERWHELMED WITHOUT ELECTRONIC SURVEILLANCE AND...

THEY GOT ONE OF MY PEOPLE, JEN. SHEILA, THE... THE AGENT WHO WAS WORKING THE GATE.

DON'T WORRY, THESE WOMEN ARE JUST LONELY AND CONFUSED. THEY'LL LET YOUR GIRL GO AS SOON AS THEY'VE FOUND SOMEONE WHO'LL *LISTEN*...

LADIES, THIS IS REPRESENTATIVE JENNIFER BROWN. I'M HERE WITH SENATOR CAVANAUGH. WE'RE NOT ARMED.

WE'D LIKE TO WORK THIS OUT *PEACEFULLY*... SO WHY DON'T YOU RELEASE YOUR HOSTAGE?

CERTAINLY... AS SOON AS YOU STOP HOLDING *CONGRESS* HOSTAGE AND LET US FINISH THE JOBS OUR HUSBANDS STARTED!

YOU'RE DAVID STAHL'S WIFE, RIGHT?

MS. STAHL, I'M AFRAID THAT WON'T BE POSSIBLE.

AND WHY THE HELL NOT?

BECAUSE WE'RE POLITICIANS, NOT *ROYALTY*.

REPRESENTATIVE BROWN, IN THE HISTORY OF CONGRESS, *FORTY-FIVE* WIDOWS HAVE ATTEMPTED TO SUCCEED THEIR LATE HUSBANDS--

--AND NOT *ONE OF THEM* FAILED. RIGHT, I'VE HEARD THAT FACTOID, TOO.

BUT WITH RESPECT, I THINK YOU'RE FORGETTING THAT ALL OF THOSE WOMEN WERE DEMOCRATICALLY *ELECTED*.

REALLY?

WHAT ABOUT YOUR *FRIEND?*

WHEN JERRY DIED IN 2000, I... I WAS *APPOINTED* SENATOR.

YES, BUT ...BUT EVEN *THAT* HAD TO BE DONE BY AN ELECTED OFFICIAL!

A *GOVERNOR!* AND NINETY PER CENT OF THEM ARE *DEAD* NOW! WHAT ARE *WE* SUPPOSED TO DO...LET OUR HUSBANDS' SEATS REMAIN EMPTY *FOREVER?*

HONESTLY, DO YOU PEOPLE HAVE ANY IDEA WHAT'S GOING ON *OUTSIDE* WASHINGTON? LOOTING AND MASS SUICIDE AND...AND *CANNIBALISM*, FOR GOD'S SAKE!

OUR CONSTITUENCIES NEED *LEADERSHIP.*

I UNDERSTAND THAT, MS. STAHL, AND WE DO INTEND TO HOLD SPECIAL ELECTIONS ...*WHEN THE TIME IS RIGHT.*

UNTIL THEN, YOU CAN DO MORE GOOD IN YOUR *COMMUNITIES* THAN YOU COULD INSIDE THE *CAPITOL!*

BLAM

BLAM BLAM BLAM

WELL, *THIS* SUCKS.

JESUS CHRIST, *PLEASE.* I'M AN ESCAPE ARTIST, NOT MAC-FUCKING-GYVER.

I CAN'T BUST OUT OF A *FORTRESS* WITH TWO PAPER CLIPS AND A...

HUH.

WE'VE GOT SMOKE DETECTORS... BUT NO FIRE-SUPPRESSION CRAP.

NO SPRINKLERS, NO CO_2...NOTHING THEY'D HAVE TO PUMP IN FROM *OUTSIDE.*

SO WHAT WERE THE DUDES WHO INSTALLED THIS SHIT *THINKING,* AMP?

IF NANCY REAGAN ACCIDENTALLY DROPPED HER JOINT IN HERE AND LIT THIS PLACE UP, WOULD THAT DOOR POP OPEN...

...OR WOULD A BUNCH OF ALARMS RING IN SOME OFF-SITE MONITORING STATION WHILE SHE *BURNED* TO DEATH?

ONE WAY TO FIND OUT.

SHINK

DON'T!

BLAM

DAMMIT!

WHY... WHY DID YOU DO THAT?

ERIN NEVER... SHE NEVER EVEN TOUCHED A GUN BEFORE. IT WAS AN ACCIDENT.

I DON'T CARE. NOW DROP THE WEAPON BEFORE I--

IT WAS AN ACCIDENT!

KABLAM

UHN!

DIANE!

JENNIFER, WAIT!

I...I'M NOT SUPPOSED TO *BE* HERE. I JUST WANTED TO GET SOME PHOTOS OUT OF KURT'S OFFICE. PHOTOS OF THE BOYS AND...

JESUS, I WRITE *COOKBOOKS*...

HOW BAD?

I'LL... LIVE.

BUT WHAT...THE HELL...

...IS *THAT?*

SORRREEEECH

DROP YOUR WEAPONS.

PLEASE.

Morris Waste Disposal

WHO THE HELL ARE *YOU*?

FORGET ABOUT *HER*...

...*I'M* THE PRESIDENT OF THE UNITED STATES.

AND I SAY DROP THE GODDAMN WEAPONS.

GET BACK INSIDE THE TRUCK, MA'AM.

MARGARET? BUT... YOU'RE THE SECRETARY OF *AGRICULTURE*.

NOT ANYMORE. NOW WHAT THE HELL IS GOING ON HERE, STAHL?

SECRETARY VALENTINE, WE...WE THOUGHT YOU WERE *DEAD*.

DON'T LISTEN TO THEM, MARGARET! THE DEMOCRATS JUST SHOT BILL WOODRING'S *WIFE*!

AFTER YOU *MURDERED* AN INNOCENT SECRET SERVICE AGENT!

YOU DON'T UNDERSTAND, WE...WE DIDN'T HAVE A *CHOICE*. THEY'VE SEIZED CONTROL OF THE WHITE HOUSE.

WE HAVEN'T *SEIZED* ANYTHING! FOR SOMEONE WHO CALLS HERSELF A REPUBLICAN, YOU DON'T SEEM TO COMPREHEND THE FACT THAT THIS IS A *REPUBLIC*.

WE RULE BY *LAW*, NOT BY THE...THE WHIMS OF ARMED *MILITIAS*!

MADAM PRESIDENT, CONGRESS HAS ONLY BEEN DOING EXACTLY WHAT THE FOUNDING FATHERS INTENDED.

THE FOUNDING FATHERS ARE *DEAD*!

ALL OF THE MEN ARE DEAD! THEIR CONSTITUTION DOESN'T *APPLY* ANYMORE!

IT'S TIME FOR SOMETHING *NEW*.

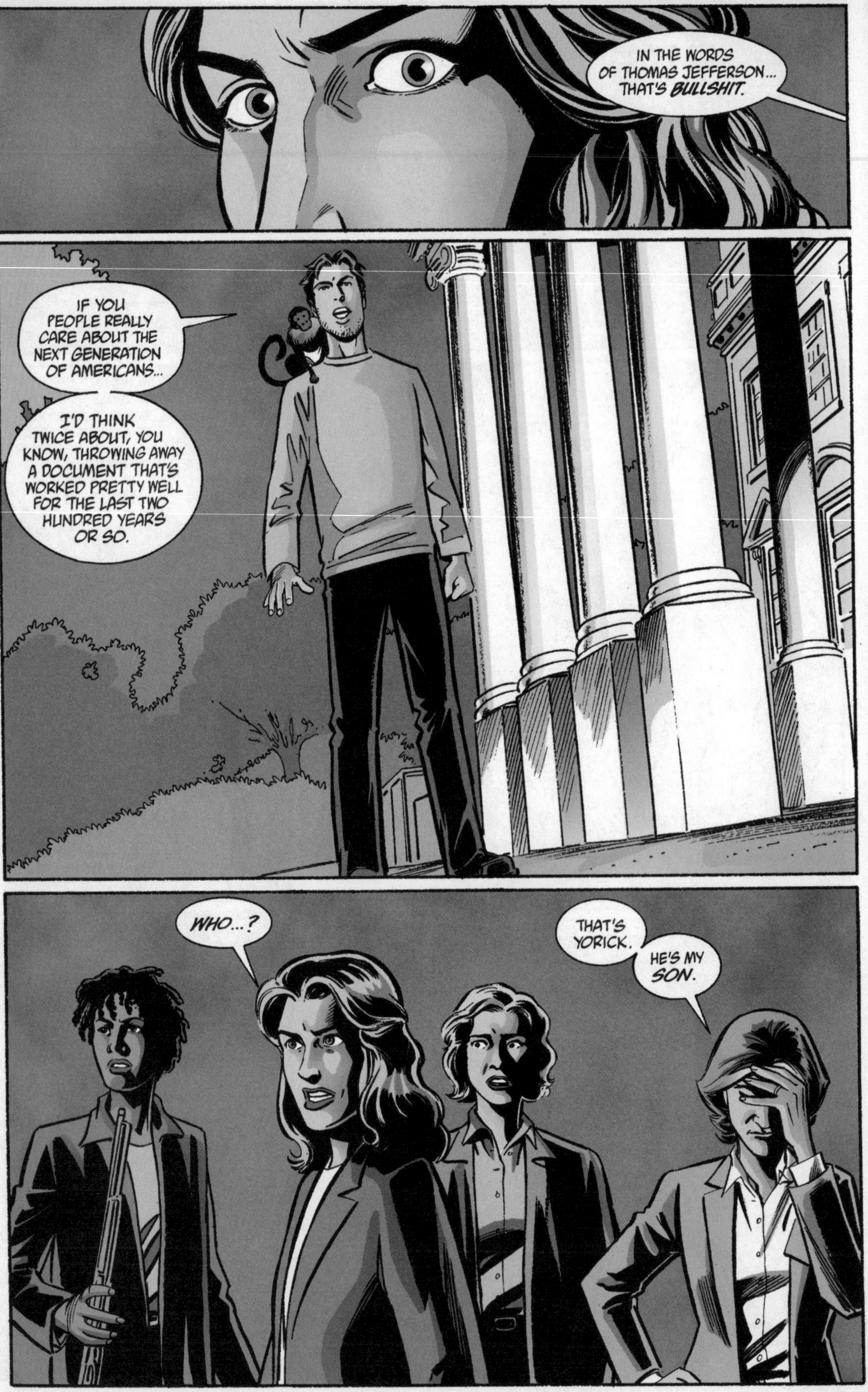

IN THE WORDS OF THOMAS JEFFERSON... THAT'S *BULLSHIT*.

IF YOU PEOPLE REALLY CARE ABOUT THE NEXT GENERATION OF AMERICANS...

I'D THINK TWICE ABOUT, YOU KNOW, THROWING AWAY A DOCUMENT THAT'S WORKED PRETTY WELL FOR THE LAST TWO HUNDRED YEARS OR SO.

WHO...?

THAT'S YORICK. HE'S MY *SON*.

I DON'T KNOW IF I'M THE *ONLY* MAN ON EARTH...BUT I SWEAR I'M NOT GOING TO BE THE *LAST.*

AND I'D HATE TO HAVE TO TELL *MY* CHILDREN THAT THIS GREAT NATION, WHICH MILLIONS OF MY BROTHERS SHED THEIR BLOOD TO FORGE, WAS COMPLETELY *UNDONE* BY--

THAT'S *ENOUGH,* YOUNG MAN.

THESE WOMEN HAVE SUFFERED MORE THAN YOU CAN IMAGINE. THEY DON'T DESERVE TO BE LECTURED TO BY A SELF-RIGHTEOUS *CHILD.*

THANK YOU, MARGARET. WE WERE ONLY TRYING TO--

OH, SHUT UP, STAHL. THE BOY'S RIGHT. YOU'RE A DISGRACE TO OUR PARTY.

AGENT 355, ARREST THESE CIVILIANS.

BUT...?

AND I'D LIKE A WORD WITH *YOU* IN MY OFFICE.

OF COURSE, MISS, UH...MISS *PRESIDENT.*

BUT FIRST...

...YOU MIGHT WANT TO DO SOMETHING ABOUT THE *INFERNO* IN YOUR BASEMENT.

...AND WHAT ABOUT THE *GARBAGE TRUCK?*

YOU'RE NOT GOING TO BELIEVE THIS, BUT 355 AND I COMMANDEERED IT FROM A *SUPER-MODEL...*

I DON'T UNDERSTAND. THE CULPER RING WAS *GEORGE WASHINGTON'S* SPY NETWORK. THEY HAVEN'T EXISTED SINCE THE *REVOLUTION.*

I WISH I COULD TELL YOU MORE, REPRESENTATIVE... BUT YOU DON'T HAVE *CLEARANCE.*

ALL RIGHT, LADIES, WE CAN FINISH OUR SMALL TALK *AFTER* THE U.S. MALE HERE TELLS US ABOUT HIS PLANS.

WELL, WITH YOUR PERMISSION, I'D LIKE TO FIND THAT BIOENGINEER MY MOTHER TOLD ME ABOUT...DO WHAT-EVER I CAN TO HELP WITH HER RESEARCH.

AFTER THAT, I, uh... PLAN TO GO ON TO *AUSTRALIA.* MY GIRLFRIEND IS THERE, MA'AM. I HAVE TO--

ABSOLUTELY NOT, YORICK.

WE WILL FIND A WAY TO BRING DR. MANN AND BETH TO YOU, BUT YOU ARE *NOT* LEAVING THE WHITE HOUSE.

MOM, I SURVIVED ON THE ROAD FOR *MONTHS* BY MYSELF...BUT I WAS IN THIS PLACE *FIFTEEN MINUTES* BEFORE IT TURNED INTO NIGHT OF THE LIVING DEAD.

YORICK'S RIGHT.

I...I AM?

IT WON'T BE LONG BEFORE OTHERS LEARN OF YOUR EXISTENCE, AND I DON'T THINK IT'S WISE TO KEEP YOU IN ONE LOCATION WHERE THEY'LL ALWAYS BE ABLE TO FIND YOU.

AT THE SAME TIME, I HAVE NO INTENTION OF LETTING THE BEST HOPE FOR OUR FUTURE HITCHHIKE ACROSS THE ENTIRE *PLANET.*

WE'LL DO EVERYTHING WE CAN TO REUNITE YOU WITH YOUR *FRIEND,* BUT AFTER YOU'VE FOUND DR. MANN, I DON'T WANT YOU LEAVING THE STATES.

AND TO MAKE *SURE* THAT YOU STAY WITHIN OUR BORDERS...I'M ASSIGNING AGENT 355 TO BE YOUR CHAPERONE.

CHAPERONE? MADAM PRESIDENT, I... I NEED TO PROTECT *YOU.* THE SECRET SERVICE--

--IS HIRING MORE GIRLS EVERY DAY. BESIDES, FINDING PEOPLE AND GETTING THEM WHERE THEY NEED TO *GO* SEEMS TO BE YOUR *SPECIALTY.*

AND HAVEN'T YOU TAKEN AN OATH TO DO WHATEVER THE COMMANDER IN CHIEF *TELLS* YOU TO DO?

YES MA'AM.

EXCELLENT. YOU'LL LEAVE AFTER YORICK'S HAD SOME TIME TO CONVINCE HIS MOTHER THAT HE'S NOT GOING TO DO ANYTHING *FOOLISH* DURING HIS JOURNEY.

THANK YOU, MA'AM.

GODSPEED TO YOU BOTH, AND WHATEVER YOU DO...

...DON'T FUCK THIS UP.

79

Tel Aviv, Israel
Three Days Later

HALO...?

IS THIS YEHUDA?

NO.

LIEUTENANT-GENERAL YEHUDA IS DEAD.

THIS IS ALTER TSE'ELON... *NEW* CHIEF OF THE GENERAL STAFF.

TO WHOM AM I SPEAKING?

THAT'S NOT IMPORTANT.

YES. IT IS.

THIS IS A DIRECT LINE TO A GOVERNMENTAL SAFE HOUSE IN THE UNITED STATES. HOW DID YOU--

NONE OF THAT MATTERS, ALTER. THE ONLY THING THAT SHOULD CONCERN YOU NOW...

...IS A YOUNG MAN NAMED YORICK BROWN.

Washington, D.C.
Now

UHN!

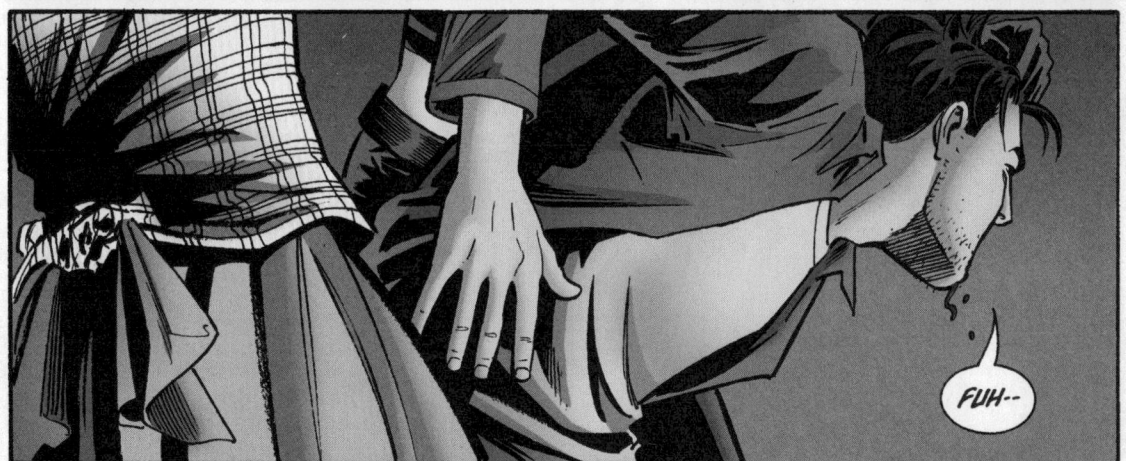

FUH--

OOF!

Washington, D.C.
One Hour Ago

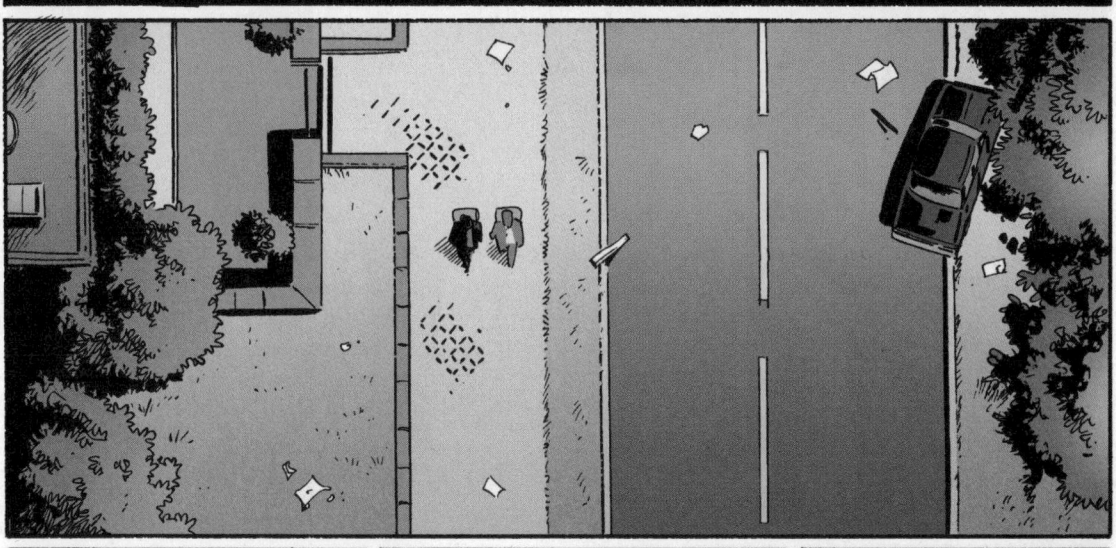

SO, uh... WHAT'S THE PLAN, FRAN?

THAT'S NOT MY NAME.

NO KIDDING. I WAS ONLY--

THERE'S A *REASON* MY REAL NAME IS CLASSIFIED, YORICK.

IF YOU HAVE TO CALL ME SOMETHING, YOU CAN CALL ME 355.

AND IF YOU'LL BE MY BODYGUARD, YOU CAN CALL ME AL?

WHAT?

FORGET IT.

WE'LL NEVER MAKE IT TO BOSTON ON FOOT, AND THE HIGHWAYS ARE TOO CONGESTED TO TRAVEL BY CAR.

WE NEED MOTORCYCLES.

GOOD LUCK. I'D HAVE AN EASIER TIME FINDING A FELLOW *THREE STOOGES* FAN.

EVER SINCE ALL THE MEN DIED, BIKES HAVE BEEN HOARDED LIKE--

I *KNOW*, YORICK. JUST... DO ME A FAVOR. PUT YOUR GAS MASK BACK ON AND STOP TALKING.

WHY DON'T *YOU* STOP TALKING?

KEEP YOUR VOICE DOWN.

NO! YOU AND I NEED TO SETTLE OUR SHIT, RIGHT HERE, RIGHT NOW.

WE BOTH KNOW THAT I RESENT YOU DRAGGING ME TO SOME ATTACK-OF-THE-CLONES DOCTOR WHEN I COULD BE OUT THERE LOOKING FOR THE GIRL I LOVE. *FINE*.

I'M SURE *YOU* RESENT HAVING TO CHAPERONE THE LAST DUDE ON EARTH WHEN YOU'D RATHER BE DOING... WHATEVER IT IS YOU DO FOR YOUR LITTLE SECRET SOCIETY.

BUT YOU KNOW WHAT? THAT'S OUR LOT IN THIS SHITTY LIFE, SO WE MIGHT AS WELL LEARN TO BE CIVIL WITH EACH OTHER WHILE WE'RE LIVING IT.

THE CULPER RING IS HARDLY A "SECRET SOCIETY." YOU CAN READ ABOUT US IN ANY HISTORY BO--

WHO CARES ABOUT YOUR STUPID *CLUB?* THAT'S ALL YOU EVER TALK ABOUT! I MEAN, DON'T YOU HAVE FRIENDS OR A... A *FAMILY?*

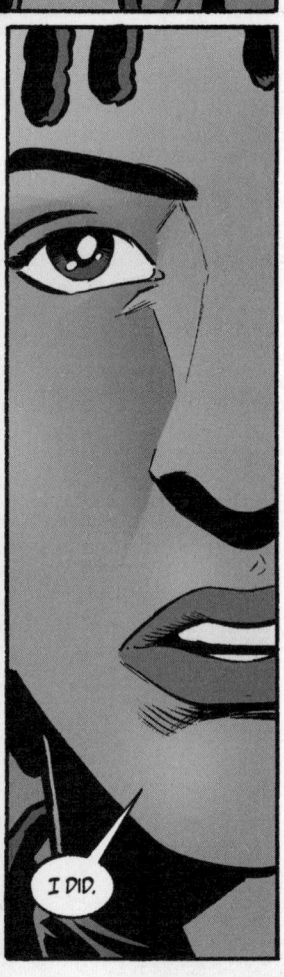

I DID.

OH. CRAP. LISTEN, 355, I--

IT'S ALL RIGHT, YORICK.

I LOST THEM A LONG TIME AGO.

HOW ABOUT YOU? YOU EVER THINK ABOUT ANYONE OTHER THAN THAT GIRLFRIEND OF YOURS?

BETH'S NOT MY GIRLFRIEND, SHE'S MY *FIANCÉE* ...SORT OF.

AND NO, SHE'S NOT THE ONLY PERSON I'M WORRIED ABOUT. I STILL HAVEN'T HEARD FROM MY BIG SISTER, HERO.

HERO?

MY DAD TEACHES...

...TAUGHT DRAMA.

I GUESS HE THOUGHT NAMING HIS KIDS AFTER OBSCURE SHAKESPEARE CHARACTERS MIGHT HELP HIM GET *TENURE*.

EITHER THAT OR HE WAS PUNISHING US FOR BEING BORN.

STILL, IN A WEIRD WAY, HERO AND I SORT OF GREW INTO OUR NAMES.

SHE GOT A GIG AS AN *EMT*... I BECAME A WORTHLESS JOKER.

YOU TWO ARE CLOSE, HUH?

LIKE LUKE AND LEIA... *um*, MINUS THE FRENCH KISSING. MY FAMILY MOVED AROUND A LOT WHEN WE WERE KIDS, SO HERO AND I WERE ALWAYS BEST FRIENDS BY DEFAULT.

ACTUALLY, I WAS HOPING YOU'D LET ME TAKE A LOOK FOR HER AFTER WE FOUND DR. MANN. LAST I HEARD, HERO WAS IN BOSTON, TOO.

WE'LL SEE, YORICK. OUR FIRST PRIORITY IS STILL--

WAIT.

WHAT THE HELL IS THAT?

AH. ALWAYS ABOUT *THAT* WITH YOU LADIES, ISN'T IT?

HEY, *WE* DIDN'T BUILD THE THING.

IS THERE ANY CHANCE I COULD PAY MY RESPECTS? JUST FOR A *MINUTE?*

I PROMISE TO STAY IN DISGUISE, 355. I CAN EVEN *SOUND* LIKE A WOMAN. WHEN I WAS IN HIGH SCHOOL, I USED TO CALL THESE PARTY LINES AND PRETEND I WAS A--

I'M SORRY, YORICK. WE CAN'T AFFORD THE RISK.

YEAH. YEAH, I UNDER-STAND.

HEY, CAN YOU HOLD ONTO AMPERSAND FOR A SECOND?

MMN MMN

NO!

YORICK, YOUR MONKEY HAS *PROBLEMS.* HE TRIED TO HAVE SEX WITH MY *ARM* LAST NIGHT! YOU CAN'T JUST...

YORICK?

OH MY GOD.

EXCUSE ME.

YOU'RE NOT A... ARE YOU A...?

OH. I...I SAW THE GAS MASK AND I THOUGHT MAYBE YOU WERE ANOTHER...

I THOUGHT MAYBE YOU WERE SOMEONE I KNEW.

I KNOW YOU, HONEY?

SORRY. JUST GOT SO USED TO WEARING THIS DAMN THING AFTER THE PLAGUE HIT, IT'S KINDA BECOME MY SECURITY BLANKET. YOU TOO, HUH?

I'M ROSE, BY THE WAY. TAKE A LOAD OFF.

THANKS. I'M...BETH.

PLEASURE. WHO ARE YOU HERE FOR TONIGHT, BETH?

ME? I...I DON'T KNOW. ALL THE GUYS I HAVEN'T SAID GOODBYE TO YET, I GUESS.

LIKE, uh...MY SEVENTH GRADE ENGLISH TEACHER? MR. FELDER? BEEN YEARS SINCE I TALKED WITH HIM...BUT YOU NEVER REALLY FORGET THE MAN WHO GIVES YOU TO KILL A MOCKINGBIRD, YOU KNOW?

HOW ABOUT YOU?

MICK JAGGER.

SERIOUSLY?

ABSOLUTELY. I MEAN, DON'T GET ME WRONG, I DON'T MISS ANYONE LIKE I MISS MY PALS, BUT IT SUDDENLY HIT ME TODAY...

THE ROLLING STONES ARE DEAD.

WHAT... WHAT DO YOU MEAN?

YOU HAVE AN INSTRUMENT?

UH... NO?

WELL YOU BETTER *GET ONE*, GIRL. WE'VE GOT TO PICK UP WHERE THE BOYS LEFT OFF. CHANNEL SOME OF THAT *JANIS MOJO.*

AH. RIGHT.

MY BAND'S TRYING TO SCRAPE ENOUGH FOOD TOGETHER TO BUY PASSAGE TO THE UK. I HEARD TORI'S STARTED SOME KIND OF COMMUNE FOR MUSICIANS OVER THERE.

HEY, IF YOU KNOW ANY DECENT DRUMMERS, WE...

OH *FUCK.*

WHAT IS IT?

THEM.

AMAZONS.

I'VE ONLY HEARD RUMORS. THEY'RE LIKE... ROVING PACKS OF PISSED-OFF LESBIANS, RIGHT?

NAH, THEY'RE NOT GAY. THEY'RE *INSANE.* SOMEONE TOLD ME THAT THEY ALL BURN ONE OF THEIR OWN BOOBS OFF.

WHY?

SUPPOSEDLY THAT'S WHAT THE *REAL* AMAZONS DID. MAKES IT EASIER TO SHOOT AN ARROW OR SOMETHING.

WHO KNOWS. SOME GIRLS WILL DO ANY RETARDED SHIT TO GET INTO A GANG, LONG AS IT MEANS FOOD AND PROTECTION.

WHAT ARE THEY *DOING?*

SAME THING THEY'VE BEEN DOING TO EVERY OTHER "SYMBOL OF THE PATRIARCHY."

WHAT-EVER, WE'LL JUST CLEAN IT UP LATER. IT'S NOT WORTH GETTING KILLED OVER. COME ON, LET'S JET.

FUCK THAT.

BETH, WAIT!

THOSE PEOPLE ARE *DANGEROUS.* YOU CAN'T...

MAN.

THAT CHICK IS *NUTS.*

GOOD RIDDANCE

Washington, D.C.
Now

...SERIOUSLY RETHINKING MY NO-HITTING-WOMEN POLICY.

ENOUGH.

I'M SORRY ABOUT THIS, BUT THE OPPRESSED HAVE NO CHOICE BUT TO RISE UP AND DESTROY THEIR--

AHHHHHH!

I'LL MISS YOU DADDY

UHN!

ALWAYS LOVE YOU

HHN.

GET THE FUCK OFF ME!

YOU'RE A DEAD MAN.

THEN STOP TALKING AND DO IT, YOU FUCKING PUSSY!

IF THIS IS YOUR WORLD, I WANT OUT. JUST GO AHEAD AND KILL ME ALREADY!

DON'T LISTEN TO HIM, MA'AM.

WHAT ARE YOU, HIS LITTLE STEPFORD WIFE?

TRUST ME, I'M DOING YOU A FAVOR.

YOU GET ONE WARNING. LET HIM GO.

PLEASE.

RAISE YOUR HAND TO ME AND I'LL OPEN YOU UP FASTER THAN--

RUN.

CUTTING IT A LITTLE CLOSE, AREN'T WE?

NOT REALLY. I'VE BEEN WATCHING YOU FOR THE LAST TEN MINUTES.

THE... WHAT ARE YOU *TALKING* ABOUT?

YOU JUST STOOD THERE WHILE THEY *BEAT* ME? *WHY?*

LOVE YOU

TO TEACH YOU A LESSON.

JUST BECAUSE YOU'VE GOT A *DICK* DOESN'T MEAN THAT YOU'RE *INVINCIBLE.*

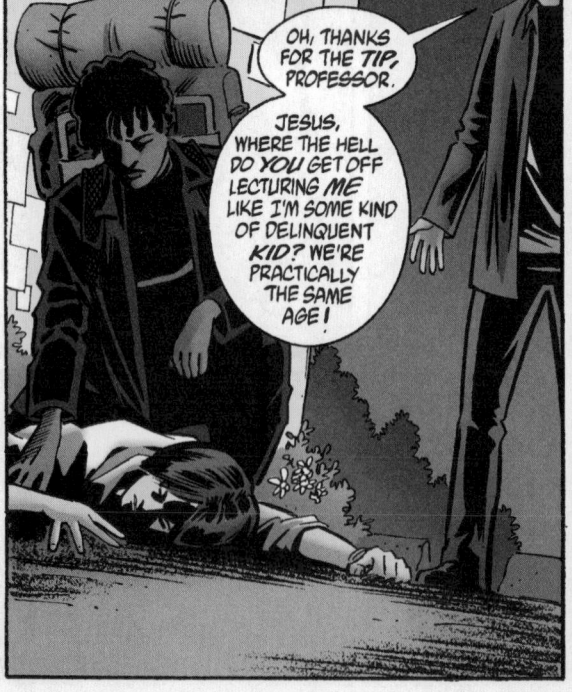

OH, THANKS FOR THE *TIP,* PROFESSOR.

JESUS, WHERE THE HELL DO *YOU* GET OFF LECTURING *ME* LIKE I'M SOME KIND OF DELINQUENT *KID?* WE'RE PRACTICALLY THE SAME AGE!

THEN START ACTING LIKE IT, YORICK!

YOU'VE BEEN ENTRUSTED WITH ONE OF THE MOST IMPORTANT MISSIONS IN *HISTORY,* AND WHAT DO YOU DO?

REVEAL YOURSELF TO YET *ANOTHER* PACK OF STRANGERS? RISK YOUR LIFE OVER SOME *PISSING CONTEST?* WHAT THE HELL WERE YOU *THINKING?*

I WAS THINKING WE NEEDED SOME MOTORCYCLES.

ALL PART OF THE PLAN... FRAN.

BEANTOWN OR BUST, RIGHT?

GONNA BE A LONG FUCKIN' RIDE...

BOBBY FISCHER ONCE SAID THAT HE COULD DEFEAT ANY WOMAN AT CHESS HANDS-DOWN...PLAYING BLIND-FOLDED AND WITHOUT HIS KNIGHTS.

I BEAT HIM IN A PRIVATE MATCH WHEN I WAS *THIRTEEN*.

HAHA HA HA HA HA

HAHA

OUR OPPONENTS ARE GONE NOW...BUT THAT DOESN'T MEAN THAT WE'VE WON.

THERE ARE MISGUIDED WOMEN OUT THERE WHO WILL ATTEMPT TO REMAKE THIS WORLD *EXACTLY* AS IT ONCE WAS. AS DAUGHTERS OF THE AMAZON, WE HAVE AN OBLIGATION TO--

VICTORIA!

VICTORIA, I'M SO SORRY, I...I FUCKED UP.

OFF YOUR KNEES, CHLOE. WE'RE ALL EQUALS HERE.

WHAT HAPPENED? ARE YOU ALL RIGHT?

A MAN, WE RAN INTO A MAN.

YOU'RE SURE? NOT ANOTHER POST-OP?

HE WAS REAL, VICTORIA. WE TRIED TO...TO DO WHAT YOU TAUGHT US TO DO ...BUT HE GOT AWAY.

DO YOU HAVE ANY IDEA WHERE HE WAS HEADED?

I HEARD HIM SAY SOMETHING ABOUT...ABOUT BOSTON.

FINE. I'LL NEED SOMEONE TO LEAD OUR SEARCH PARTY. ARE ANY OF YOU FAMILIAR WITH THE AREA?

I AM.

THANK YOU, LOVE.

FORGIVE ME, YOU'RE NEW, AREN'T YOU? YOUR NAME?

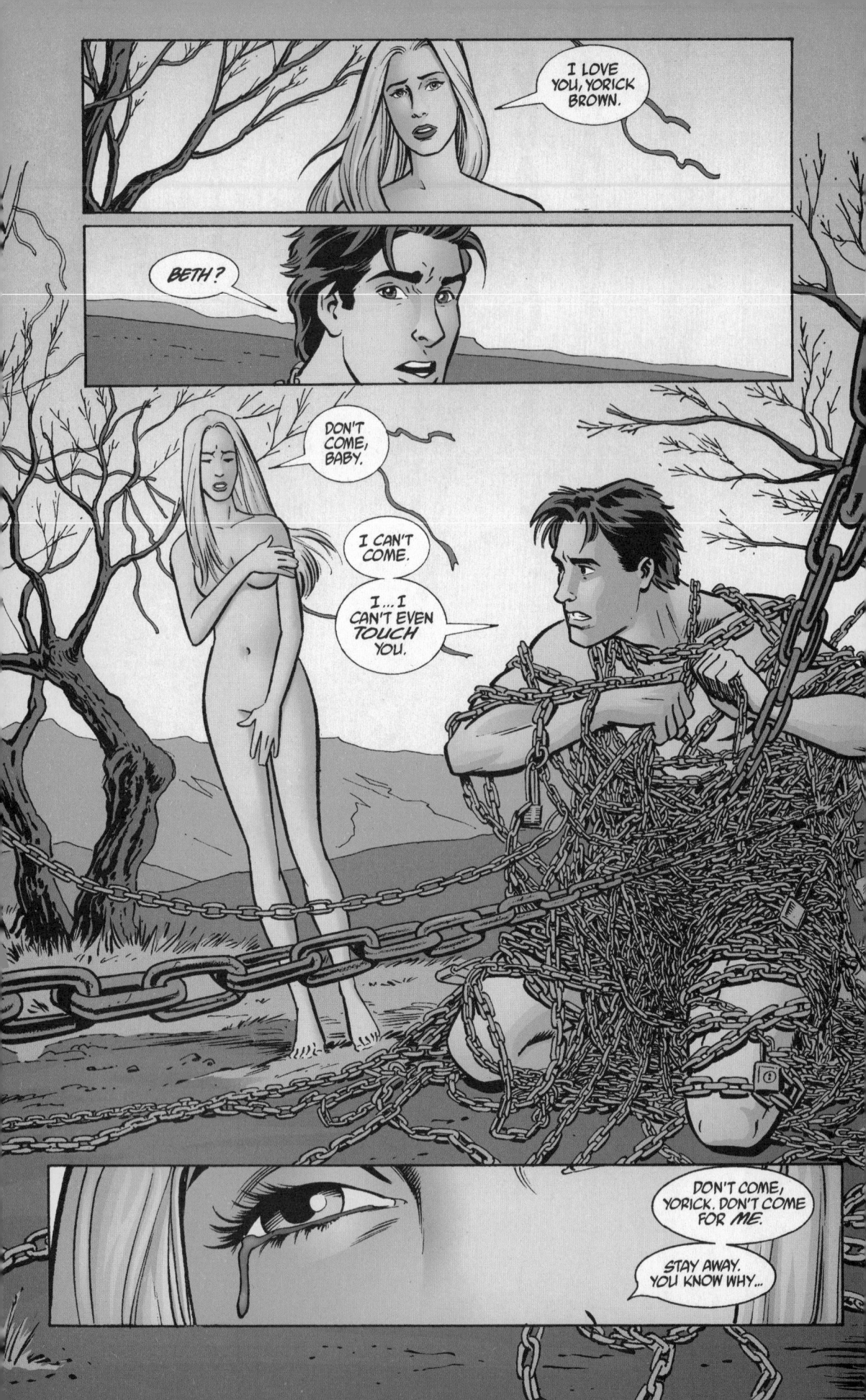

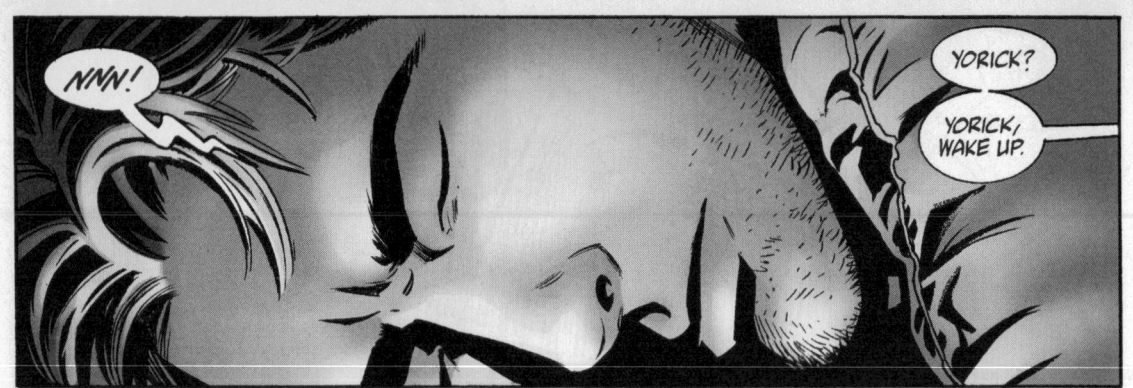

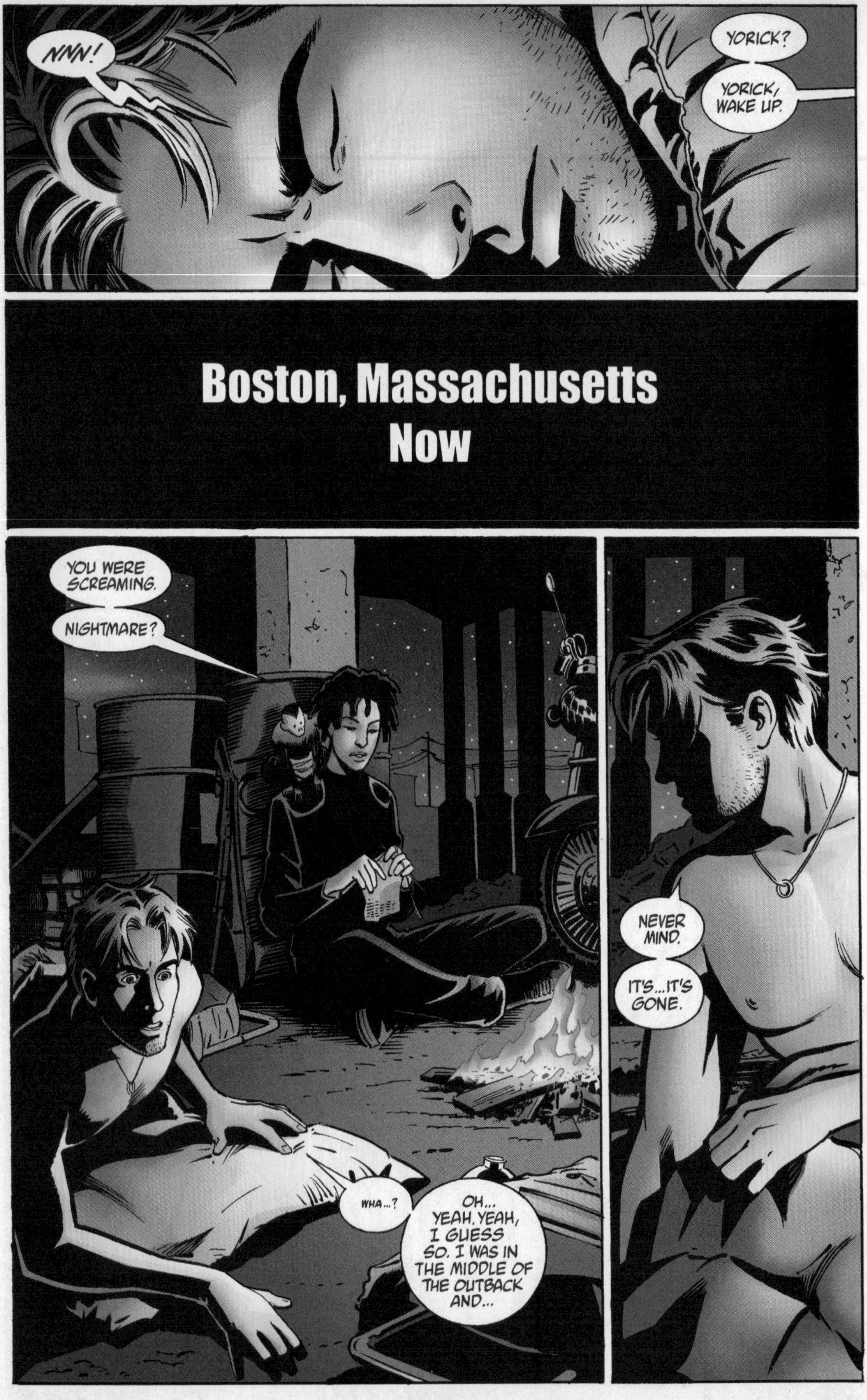

NNN!

YORICK?

YORICK, WAKE UP.

Boston, Massachusetts
Now

YOU WERE SCREAMING.

NIGHTMARE?

NEVER MIND.

IT'S...IT'S GONE.

WHA...?

OH... YEAH. YEAH, I GUESS SO. I WAS IN THE MIDDLE OF THE OUTBACK AND...

108

MORE IMPORTANT... ARE YOU *KNITTING*?

SO?

I DIDN'T THINK YOU *HAD* HOBBIES, 35S. OTHER THAN, YOU KNOW, CLEANING GUNS AND SHARPENING KNIVES AND... WELL, GENERALLY FIDGETING WITH THINGS THAT *KILL PEOPLE*.

MY GRAND-MOTHER TAUGHT ME. IT'S JUST SOMETHING I DO WHEN I GET...

IT'S JUST SOMETHING TO KEEP MY *HANDS* BUSY.

WHAT ARE YOU WORKING ON... RIFLE COZY?

THESE THINGS CAN KILL PEOPLE TOO, YOU KNOW.

ANYWAY, IT'S GOOD YOU'RE AWAKE. AS LONG AS THE SUN IS DOWN, YOU AND I CAN KEEP SEARCHING FOR DR. MANN.

WHY DO WE HAVE TO DO EVERYTHING IN THE MIDDLE OF THE NIGHT? I MEAN, NO ONE LOOKS AT ME TWICE WHEN I'VE GOT *THIS THING* ON.

I'VE SINGLE-HANDEDLY DISPROVED THE EXISTENCE OF "GUYDAR."

THIS IS *SOUTHIE*, YORICK. YOU MIGHT BE ABLE TO LOOK LIKE A LADY... BUT I CAN'T LOOK *WHITE*.

YOU SERIOUSLY THINK THAT'S STILL AN ISSUE?

WHY, BECAUSE THIS IS THE TWENTY-FIRST CENTURY... OR BECAUSE ALL OF THE MEN ARE DEAD? EITHER WAY, MY ANSWER IS YES.

FAIR ENOUGH.

HEY, BEFORE WE GO ON ANOTHER MANN-HUNT, CAN WE TAKE ONE LAST LOOK FOR HERO?

I'M SORRY, YORICK... I...I DON'T KNOW WHAT ELSE WE CAN DO. I TOLD YOU, I CHECKED YOUR SISTER'S APARTMENT, THE FIRE-HOUSE, HER BOYFRIEND'S PLACE...

JESUS, HER *BOYFRIEND*...

WHAT IS IT?

I HADN'T EVEN THOUGHT ABOUT HIM. I MEAN, SHE'D ONLY BEEN DATING THE GUY FOR TWO MONTHS OR SO, BUT HE GENUINELY SEEMED LIKE A GOOD DUDE.

HERO'S ALWAYS HAD SHITTY LUCK WITH RELATION-SHIPS. EVER SINCE SHE WAS A KID, IT'S BEEN THIS CONSTANT PARADE OF LOSERS AND, YOU KNOW ...QUASI-ABUSIVE *SCUM-BAGS*.

AND JUST WHEN SHE FINDS MR. RIGHT...

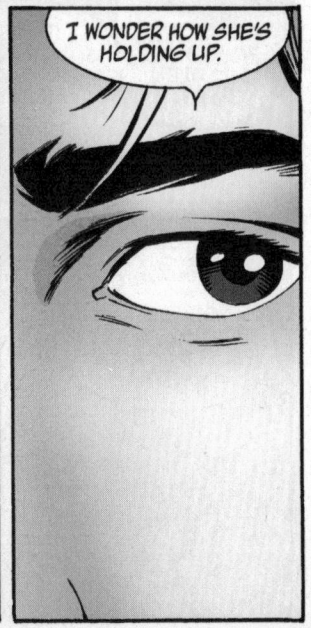

I WONDER HOW SHE'S HOLDING UP.

> **I FOUND HER.**

Putnam, Connecticut
Now

> **SHE WAS HIDING IN THE WOODS, VICTORIA.**

> **WELL, YOU GAVE US QUITE A CHASE, SISTER. YOU'RE JUST LUCKY *HERO* FOUND YOU BEFORE ONE OF MY MORE... *ZEALOUS* COMPANIONS DID.**

> **TELL ME, WHERE IN THE WORLD DID YOU GET THIS MOTORCYCLE? IT USED TO BELONG TO *US*.**

> **GO FUCK YOURSELF, YOU AMAZON *CUNT*.**

HOLD.

YOU SAY THAT WORD WITH SUCH VENOM. *CUNT.*

IT'S A FAIRLY HARMLESS INSULT IN THE UK, YOU REALIZE. ONLY IN *THIS* COUNTRY COULD A EUPHEMISM FOR FEMALE GENITALIA BE CONSIDERED THE ULTIMATE *OBSCENITY.*

THE WORD IS ACTUALLY QUITE BEAUTIFUL, RELATED TO *CUNINA,* THE ROMAN GODDESS WHO PROTECTS SLEEPING INFANTS. IT MEANS ALL-KNOWING, *ALL-POWERFUL.*

OF COURSE, *MEN* ATTEMPTED TO ROB US OF CUNT'S ANCIENT MAGIC BY MAKING THE WORD *TABOO.*

NOW THAT THE BEASTS ARE FINALLY GONE, IT'S TIME WE *RECLAIM* OUR PROPER TITLE.

DON'T FEAR WHAT YOU ARE, SISTER... *EMBRACE* IT.

I MIGHT BE A CUNT...

SpTOO

...BUT YOU'RE JUST A *BITCH.*

HERO... *KILL* THIS WHORE.

JESUS... JUST TELL HER WHERE YOU GOT THE BIKE, KID.

I...I BOUGHT IT FROM TWO WOMEN, OKAY? ONE OF THEM WAS WEARING A...A *GAS MASK*. THEY HAD AN EXTRA RIDE, SO I TRADED THEM SOME FOOD AND FUEL FOR IT.

AFTER THAT, THEY HEADED NORTH AND--

I *SAID*, KILL HER, HERO.

BUT VICTORIA, SHE MIGHT KNOW MORE ABOUT THE MAN WE'RE TRYING TO--

WE *HAVE* WHAT WE NEED. ARE YOU LOYAL TO OUR CAUSE OR NOT?

YOU *KNOW* I AM.

I DON'T KNOW *ANYTHING* ABOUT YOU, HERO. PERHAPS YOU'RE JUST ANOTHER PRO-MALE INTERLOPER, *POSING* AS A TRUE DAUGHTER OF THE AMAZON.

NOW KILL THE GIRL... OR KILL *YOURSELF.*

BLAAM

WELL PLAYED, LOVE.

BELIEVE ME, I DESPISE BARKING ORDERS LIKE A PATRIARCH. REST ASSURED, WHEN THE GAME IS OVER, THE QUEEN AND PAWN GO BACK INTO THE SAME BOX.

SADDLE UP, MY SISTERS!

SOMEWHERE OUT THERE, THE LAST OF OUR OPPRESSORS STILL LIVES!

WELL, YOU'RE HANDY WITH THE HOUDINI SHIT, I'LL GIVE YOU THAT.

HOUDINI BUSTED *OUT* OF STUFF, NOT *INTO* IT.

BESIDES, THAT GUY IS *SO* OVERRATED. NOW HARRY'S BROTHER *DASH...THERE* WAS AN ESCAPE ARTIST WHO COULD ACTUALLY--

YOUR MOTHER SAID DR. MANN LISTED THIS LAB AS A PRIMARY WORK ADDRESS ON HER LAST W-2.

WE'RE LOOKING FOR A PALM PILOT, ROLODEX, *SOMETHING* TO TELL US WHERE SHE MIGHT HAVE GONE.

NOT INTERESTED IN THE GREAT HARDEEN, HUH? KIDS THESE DAYS...

HEY, I'VE BEEN MEANING TO ASK, DID THIS "CULPER RING" YOU WORK FOR LET YOU PICK YOUR *OWN* JAMES BOND NUMBER, OR WAS THERE SOME KINDA LOTTERY TO--

SHH.

SOMEONE'S HERE.

HELLO?

DR. ALLISON MANN?

RAAAAH!

UHN!

WHAT...WHAT THE HELL DO YOU *WANT?* IF YOU'RE LOOKING FOR *DRUGS,* YOU PICKED THE WRONG--

DOCTOR, MY NAME IS AGENT 355. I WAS SENT TO FIND YOU BY THE UNITED STATES GOVERNMENT.

YOU'RE HERE TO *ARREST* ME?

NO, MA'AM. I'M HERE TO *ASSIST* YOU...WITH YOUR CLONING RESEARCH.

REALLY? WELL YOU CAN TELL THE GOVERNMENT THAT I'M *DONE* WITH CLONING.

THEN...WHAT ARE YOU WORKING ON NOW?

A CURE FOR BREAST CANCER.

FORGIVE ME, DOCTOR, BUT ISN'T THAT A BIT LIKE REARRANGING DECK CHAIRS ON THE *TITANIC?*

IF WE'RE GOING TO BE THE *LAST* GENERATION OF HUMANS, WE SHOULD AT LEAST BE ALLOWED TO LIVE OUT OUR MISERABLE LIVES IN *GOOD HEALTH.*

BUT...IF YOU COULD FIND A WAY TO *CLONE* A HUMAN, WE WOULDN'T HAVE TO *BE* THE LAST GENERATION.

I TOLD YOU, I AM *FINISHED* WITH CLONING. I JUST WANT TO DO WHATEVER I CAN TO MAKE UP FOR MY STUPID MISTAKE ...SO I CAN *KILL* MYSELF IN GOOD CONSCIENCE.

WAIT, *WHAT* MISTAKE?

MY CHILD.

HE'S WHAT GOT US INTO THIS MESS.

WHAT ARE YOU TALKING ABOUT?

BEFORE THE UMBILICAL WAS EVEN SEVERED, THE CLONE I GAVE BIRTH TO SOMEHOW... *DESTROYED* EVERY LAST SPERM, FETUS AND FULLY DEVELOPED MAMMAL WITH A *Y* CHROMOSOME.

OR MAYBE YOU HADN'T NOTICED.

YOU...YOU *ALREADY* CLONED A HUMAN BEING?

HE WASN'T JUST "A HUMAN BEING," HE WAS MY *NEPHEW*.

MY BROTHER'S SON WAS DYING OF LEUKEMIA. HE NEEDED A BONE MARROW TRANSPLANT. WE COULDN'T FIND A MATCHING DONOR... SO I DECIDED TO *CREATE* ONE.

MY TEAM AND I FAST-TRACKED OUR RESEARCH AND FINALLY MANAGED TO FUSE ONE OF THE BOY'S SKIN CELLS WITH AN EMPTY DONOR EGG. AND THEN I IMPREGNATED *MYSELF*.

IT WAS MORE COMPLICATED THAN THAT... BUT NOT BY MUCH. "IMMACULATE CONCEPTION FOR DUMMIES," MY PARTNER CALLED IT.

IT'S FUNNY. WE USED TO LAUGH AT THE CHRISTIAN WACKOS WHO SAID WE'D BE PUNISHED FOR PLAYING GOD. BUT NOW...

DOCTOR, YOU...YOU CAN'T BE *SURE* THAT CLONING CAUSED THE PLAGUE. *EVERY* WOMAN THINKS SHE DID SOMETHING TO CONTRIBUTE TO... WHAT HAPPENED, EVEN ME. IT'S CALLED *SURVIVOR'S SYNDROME*, AND--

IT'S NOT A GODDAMN *SYNDROME*! THIS IS *MY FAULT*!

ONE MINUTE, MY...MY *BABY* WAS TAKING HIS LAST BREATH, AND THE NEXT, ALL OF THE MEN ARE *DEAD*!

NOT ALL OF THEM...

WHAT'S UP, DOC?

OH MY GOD.

I GET THAT A LOT.

THE SIZE OF THOSE CANINES. IS THIS MONKEY A *MALE*?

uh...YEAH. ACTUALLY, I'M *ALSO*--

OBVIOUSLY. WHERE DID YOU FIND THIS ANIMAL?

AMPERSAND? HE FOUND *ME.* I VOLUNTEERED TO TRAIN A HELPER MONKEY A FEW MONTHS AGO, AND SOME GROUP FROM OUT HERE SENT ME THIS GUY.

HE'S GOT A LONG WAY TO GO BEFORE YOU COULD REALLY CALL HIM *HELPFUL* THOUGH. AMPERSAND'S MORE LIKE THAT EVIL MONKEY FROM *MONKEY SHINES,* OR THE NAZI MONKEY FROM *RAIDERS,* OR THE--

I COULD UNDERSTAND *ONE* OF YOU BEING SOME KIND OF ANOMALY ...BUT HOW DID YOU *BOTH* SURVIVE?

WE WERE HOPING *YOU* COULD EXPLAIN THAT, DOCTOR.

IT DOESN'T MAKE ANY SENSE, UNLESS...

MAYBE I *DIDN'T* CAUSE THE PLAGUE. MAYBE *YOU* DID.

EXCUSE ME? PAGING DR. FRANKENSTEIN! *I'M* NOT THE ONE WHO COMMITTED CRIMES AGAINST *NATURE!*

THAT'S *ENOUGH,* YORICK.

NO ONE'S TRYING TO ASSIGN BLAME. WE'RE JUST LOOKING FOR ANSWERS.

YES, WELL... I'LL NEED TO DRAW SOME BLOOD FROM YOU AND YOUR PET.

HOLD ON, DOC. THE MONKEY'S NOT EXACTLY *OODGAY* WITH *EEDLESNAY.*

DON'T WORRY, WE USED CAPUCHINS FOR A LOT OF OUR EARLY EXPERIMENTS. I'M ACTUALLY QUITE GOOD WITH--

EEEEEEE

AMPERSAND, NO!

DON'T LET HIM GET OUTSIDE!

120

OH, FUCK! HE'S HALFWAY DOWN THE BLOCK ALREADY!

WHERE'S THE NEAREST EXIT?

FOLLOW ME!

LAST TIME HE DID THIS, IT TOOK US *THREE HOURS* TO FIND HIM!

SHUT UP AND RUN, YORICK!

Four Hours Later

SHALOM...?

⟨THERE'S NO ONE HERE.⟩

⟨YES, I CAN SEE THAT.⟩

⟨MY GOD, ALTER, HOW MUCH OF OUR NATION'S RESOURCES DID WE *WASTE* COMING TO THE STATES?⟩

⟨AND *WHY?* BECAUSE SOME ANONYMOUS AMERICAN TOLD YOU WE'D FIND A REAL-LIVE *BOY* HERE?⟩

⟨I'M FAMILIAR WITH YOUR OBJECTIONS, SADIE.⟩

⟨THIS GENERATOR IS STILL HALF FULL.⟩

⟨HE LEFT RECENTLY.⟩

⟨HOW DO YOU KNOW IT WAS A *HE?*⟩

⟨BECAUSE *SHE*s DON'T WEAR BOOTS IN A SIZE FORTY-FIVE.⟩

〈YOU'RE... YOU'RE RIGHT.〉

〈SHOCKING.〉

〈WE SHOULD STAY OUT OF SIGHT UNTIL HE RETURNS.〉

〈NO.〉

〈HE OBVIOUSLY DEPARTED IN A HURRY, LIKELY BECAUSE HE HEARD US COMING. WE NEED TO *FIND* HIM...BEFORE SOMEONE ELSE DOES.〉

〈WHAT ABOUT ALL OF THIS? ASSUMING YOUR SOURCE WAS TELLING THE TRUTH, THERE MIGHT BE INFORMATION ABOUT CREATING *MORE* MEN IN HERE.〉

〈RIGHT. IF THE ENEMY EVER GOT THEIR HANDS ON SUCH KNOWLEDGE ...THEY COULD ESSEN-TIALLY *RESURRECT* THEIR ARMIES.〉

〈I'M NOT TALKING ABOUT THE *ENEMY*, ALTER. I'M TALKING ABOUT THE FUTURE OF *ISRAEL*.〉

〈AS AM I.〉

〈SO WHAT SHOULD WE DO? CONFISCATE EVERYTHING IN THE LAB?〉

〈NO, SADIE...〉

SIRFI ET ZEH AD HA-YESOD.

Boston, Massachusetts
Six Hours Later

JESUS CHRIST, IS THAT THE *SUN* COMING UP?

I GOTTA GET A FUCKIN' *LEASH* FOR THIS THING...

ANYWAY, WHAT'S THE PLAN NOW THAT CHIM CHIM HERE IS SAFELY IN CUSTODY?

TESTS. THE PROVERBIAL *BARRAGE*, I'M AFRAID.

FIRST, I'LL NEED TO HARVEST SOME OF YOUR DENDRITIC CELLS AND COMPARE THEM TO MY CHILD'S. THANKFULLY, I HAVE SAMPLES STORED IN MY...

...LAB?

NO.

DID...DID ONE OF US LEAVE A BUNSEN BURNER ON OR SOME-THING?

THE FIRE DIDN'T TOUCH ANY OF THE NEIGHBORING BUILDINGS, THIS WAS DELIB-ERATE.

BUT...WHO WOULD WANT TO TORCH THIS PLACE? AMAZONS?

I'M NOT SURE, BUT WE HAVE TO GET OUT OF HERE. NOW.

AND GO WHERE, 355?

MY ORDERS WERE TO RETURN TO THE WHITE HOUSE IF WE RAN INTO ANY TROUBLE.

BUT THOSE BIKER CHICKS PROBABLY FOLLOWED US FROM WASHINGTON. THEY'LL BE EXPECT-ING US TO GO BACK THERE. WE CAN'T JUST--

TWELVE YEARS' WORTH OF RESEARCH ...GONE.

HEY, DON'T SWEAT IT, DOC. YOU HAVE BACKUP OF ALL YOUR SHIT... RIGHT?

I CAN RETRIEVE SOME OF MY DATA, BUT WITH-OUT EMBRYONIC SPEC-IMENS FOR REFERENCE ...THERE'S NO GUARANTEE THAT MY NEXT EXPERI-MENT WON'T KILL EVERY LAST WOMAN.

DOCTOR, DON'T MOST SCIENTISTS KEEP DUPLICATE SAMPLES IN A...A...?

A CONTINGENCY SITE? YES.

WELL, WHERE'S YOURS?

CALIFORNIA.

SO WHAT ARE WE SUPPOSED TO DO, TAKE DR. MANN ACROSS THE ENTIRE COUNTRY ON OUR *ONE* MOTOR-CYCLE?

AND HOW DO WE KNOW SOME-ONE HASN'T ALREADY BURNED DOWN THIS OTHER JOINT?

WHAT ARE YOU SUGGESTING, YORICK?

I THINK WE SHOULD ALL GO TO NEW YORK...AND BUY PASSAGE TO *AUSTRALIA*. GET AS FAR AWAY AS POSSIBLE FROM WHOEVER WANTS US *DEAD*.

BESIDES, MY GIRLFRIEND IS DOWN UNDER AND...I'M SORRY, DOC, BUT MAYBE MAKING BABIES THE *OLD-FASHIONED* WAY IS STILL OUR BEST BET. YOU TWO DON'T HAVE TO COME ALONG, BUT IT'S WHAT I--

DON'T BE AN IDIOT.

FROM HERE ON OUT, WHATEVER THE THREE OF US DO, WE DO *TOGETHER*.

FIGURED YOU'D SAY THAT.

SO WHAT'S IT GONNA BE, SCARECROW? WE TAKING THE YELLOW BRICK ROAD TO D.C., CALI...OR ALL THE WAY TO OZ?

I'M THINKING, YORICK...

I'M THINKING...

126

BRIAN K. VAUGHAN AND PIA GUERRA'S SAGA OF YORICK BROWN, THE LAST MAN ON EARTH, UNFOLDS IN THESE COLLECTIONS AVAILABLE FROM VERTIGO.

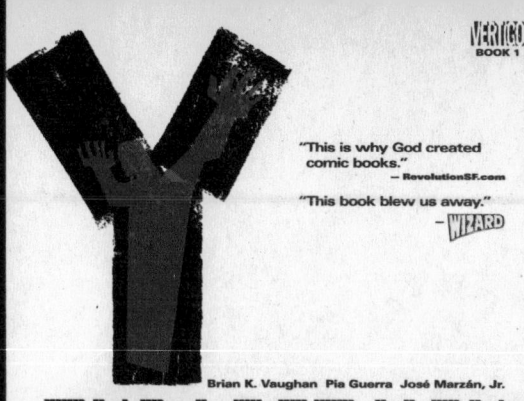

"This is why God created comic books."
— RevolutionSF.com

"This book blew us away."
— WIZARD

"A SERIOUSLY FUNNY, NUANCED FABLE...**A**"
— *ENTERTAINMENT WEEKLY*

"HAS STEADILY PROVED TO BE ONE OF THE BEST EXAMPLES OF ITS ART FORM... FASCINATING."
— *THE CHICAGO TRIBUNE*

"COMPLETE AND UTTER COMIC GOLD."
— *PUBLISHERS WEEKLY* (starred review)

Y: THE LAST MAN VOL. 1 — UNMANNED

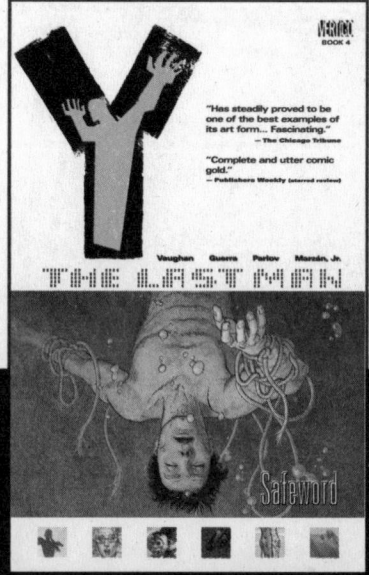

SEARCH THE GRAPHIC NOVELS SECTION OF

www.VERTIGOCOMICS.com

FOR ART AND INFORMATION ON ALL OF OUR BOOKS!